A M
OF SWINE

*Swee Continue to follow
in the Holy Council of
God. He has plans for
you.*

Walter H. Brown
6/30/18

WALTER H. BROWN

DENVER, COLORADO

Outskirts Press, Inc.
http://www.outskirtspress.com

ISBN: 978-1-4787-3278-5

Outskirts Press and the "OP" logo are trademarks belonging to Outskirts Press, Inc.

PRINTED IN THE UNITED STATES OF AMERICA

ACKNOWLEDGMENTS

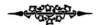

First, I thank God who has given me the courage to write this book.

I dedicate this book to my darling wife, Carol, who assisted me in every way and encouraged me while taking on this task.

My gratitude to Mrs. Angela Cerna for her friendship. May God continue to anoint her life.

INTRODUCTION

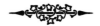

This unusual drama is poised in ambush to bludgeon the naïveté that might take it for granted that these events which are about to unfold will simply stop short within the settings where they all began: a rigorous environment, sweltering temperatures, at times remotely distant from what we call anything resembling so called modern civilization, gross poverty, relegating illiteracy, delicate lives, looming diseases, caused often by a lack of sanitary convenience and a grinning hideousness that was forced through some tiny seed of human dignity to give sprout to the astounding beauty of moral courage.

This book expresses powerful emotions about the author's shattered dream of Africa, what he had observed and experienced during his ten-year tenure there. While there was plenty of time for retrospect, he nostalgically reflects back to his native America, comparing mental notes.

As a Black man of African descent, the author shows that while certain African Americans in the past had fanaticized, in fact trivialized superficially about Africa and its multi-culture, so little has been done to their credit to discover or to get involved with what was actually occurring there.

Who would dare plunge themselves into the poverty, suffering and hardship that rested like an infested blanket over the inhabitants south of the Sahara? If they really knew, would they involve themselves in the struggle?

As for the author, it was not the romance of the glorious African past that lured him there.

The great pyramids and the Zimbabwe ruins could be seen but once. After being staggered by their magnificence and grandeur, it would all be over and applauded merely as a grand tour. But the compelling aspect was the perpetual experience of involvement, interacting with the masses, enamored with the true struggle for raw existence.

All of the elements aforementioned are personified in this true life story, *A Mourner of Swine.*

Here, we will be swept into the life of a wealthy, shrewd, and unscrupulous African Chief who held within the clutches of his greedy hands the well-being of those who are helpless about him.

TABLE OF CONTENTS

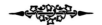

CHAPTER 1

NOT SO TOUGH DECISION

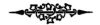

It was a cold, frost bitten, wind howling night during an unforgettable December, 1976 when my cousin, Avery, so full of excitement and equally skilled with persuasion, encouraged me to abandon everything and everybody and fly out with him to Africa. It was a dream come true. For the quest for adventure was in my blood.

"But how am I going to pay for all of this?" I asked. "For me to drop everything just to pursue a dream, I'd never be able to recover...."

Avery barged in. "Don't you worry about it, man. I'll take care of it, I've got it all planned."

Avery was quite an accomplished young man, a college graduate with a degree in economics, but he wasn't content with that. He had gone on to delve into a scientific inquiry that he called "numeric solutions to the numeric composition of diseases." To Avery, every discrepancy within physical biology could be potentially solved by a numerical solution. All of that of course was over my head and I never tried to make any sense of it, but it apparently made plenty of sense to those scientist who were attracted to it, especially because of its connections to an ancient science.

After receiving a patent for his research, Avery contracted it out to a bio-chemical research institution. That was the business venture that put him over the top.

Avery had acquired a love for travel. He had often recounted how miserable he was while attending college. To him, traveling was his education. He would much rather be exploring the pyramids or the colossus of Abu Simbel than to be stuck in a class. He nevertheless completed his academics and then went on to travels.

I was overwhelmed beyond description when one day Avery showed me a photograph of himself standing beside the tomb of Cyrus the Great, a man whom God had given his name two hundred years before his birth. There Avery stood in the Iranian atmosphere, clothed in their customary regalia. I glared with envy at the photograph.

Avery made one thing quite clear. "Look, cousin, I have no intention on staying permanently in Africa. I love the place but I've got to keep moving. I've got big business back here in the states…dead lines to meet, in fact. I'll probably be in Africa for about two months."

Avery was a "man on the move." He was also quite eccentric. He moved at a faster pace. Of course he was much younger than I. I even recalled babysitting him a couple of times. Now, he had moved past me economically, at least. That is the way it should be. We adults should never stand in the way. We should see younger people as the capsules on the tip of a rocket. After it has been launched, it falls back to the earth, but it catapults the capsule on out into interstellar space.

"I did recall hearing you say quite a few times that you would like to live in Africa someday, right?" Avery paused, then asked, "It wasn't just wishful thinking, was it?"

"No, no!" I responded. "It's not wishful thinking, cousin. It's just that it is all coming so suddenly." I thought it over. It really didn't take much thought. It was not such a tough decision. I needed a change in my life. I was confident that I had enough academics to sustain me. Besides, I had grown disenchanted with the idea of ever succeeding in America. I wanted to know what it would be like not to be treated as a second class citizen in a country that claims nominal equality for all citizens, or at least where all citizens are claimed to be equal but in time societal insanity bent the rules. Some rules became more equal than others. In all honesty, it was becoming obnoxious.

In addition to the increasing crime at the hands of fellow blacks, I was more than ready to fulfill my dream and lose myself in the masses of Africa. Come hell or high water, I was going to attempt to make a life of it. Although I had absolutely no idea of what I was inviting into my life. I remain resolved in my decisions. Dare devil that I was, it was either now or never. "Step on off into the abyss."

CHAPTER 2

MAMA ACROSS THE ALLEY

Among the many friends who attempted to persuade me to stay on in the states, was an elderly woman whom I knew only as "Mama across the alley." I had known her since my earliest childhood, but it never occurred to me to ask her name. I am sure that my own mother knew what her name was but it would not have done me any good to know what it was any, way because back in those early days children didn't just go around calling the old folks by their first name that is, if they didn't want to get "slapped back into breakfast."

Mama lived across Vanhorn Alley from us in a tiny second floor apartment at the back of the building. She could often be seen from our back yard sitting in her window looking down on us kids as we played and more than often we were throwing bricks at the rats that populated the alley.

There was one story that we had often heard Mama tell about her deceased husband who fought in World War I. One day while in the heat of a battle, Mama's husband walked upon a German soldier crouched in a prenatal position down inside of a fox hole. He looked as though he was frightened out of his wits. Mama's husband raised his rifle to shoot him, but the soldier begged him so pitifully to be spared that Mama's husband couldn't find it in his heart to do it, so he let him go.

A few days had passed when the situation was in the reverse. The Nazi soldier walked upon Mama's husband who recognized the man. He also plead with the man to spare his life and he did. It merely demonstrated that there is no war in mercy, but there can be mercy in war.

Mama's husband died and left her penniless. She was quite illiterate and had to survive on anything that she could. Neighbors assisted her whenever they could, but everybody was hard up and making it the best way that they could. In spite of it all, Mama remained a warm and gentle woman.

"Aficka!" She blurted out and reared back in surprise as far as her bent over age would allow. "Lawd, child you is jist like yo daddy, allays travlin. Why you wanna go wey ober dere to dat place? Ain't dat whare all dem lionses en stuff is?"

"Yes, Mama. There are plenty of lions in Africa." I answered. "But I'll be all right."

Mama wore a pitiful look. "Child, sompin gonna jump pout dem bushes ober dere en grabe bue. Dey gonna eat yo butt fa supper."

"Oh, Mama, I don't think that they would do any harm to me."

"Lawd, I memba when you wasn't dry behind de ears,"

she would say. "I use ta give you candy, worry yo Mama to def, cryin bout 'I wanna go see Mama-across de alley!' Now here you is talkin bout you goin to Aficka." She paused. Then she commented. "But why you wanna go messin round wey ober dare fa, boy? I think you bedder have yo head examined."

"Yes, Mama, I replied respectfully. "But I want to know more about my brothers over there."

Mama looked up at me again from over the top of her bifocals. She cocked her little flower feathered hat to one side of her head and ask "You mean to tell me dat dere ain't enough black folks ober on dis side o' de world fo you to know more bout? If'n de good Lawd ment fa us colo-lit folks to be in Aficka, He woulda kept pus s'all ober dare in de fus place."

I knew that Mama across the alley meant well, and that to a great extent she was right. She was trying in the best way that she knew how to discourage me from leaving, but I had to go. Destiny was calling. I can see her bent over figure now as I last remembered seeing her, toddling like an infant down through Van Horn Alley, between the tall red and grey brick buildings of the ghetto. An old sweet African American woman who had almost forgotten that she was an African, surviving on whatever she could find, once in a while stopping to peer into a garbage can or two, carrying an old corker sack in one hand and her twisted walking stick in the other, skewing away alley cats and throwing tin cans at rats. And there she went, a memory that can never possibly fade…Mama across the alley.

CHAPTER 3

THOUGHTS ON A PLANE

When recalling the memories of my late father who was born at the turn of the twentieth century, I was reminded of how he described his father's stories of the Marcus Garvey days and of how certain "Negros" that were involved in the movement aimed at returning black men back to Africa, reached out to recruit Grandpa, but he refused to join the Garvey Exodus. The stories of that movement lived through the years in the heart of my father, and although he could never forget it, his preoccupation with the events of life, served as preventing of his ever being able to accomplish living in Africa or going to visit it.

"Well Dad," I thought posthumously. "I'm going to give it a try. Yes sir! Perhaps you would think me nuts considering that things are far better for black men in America today than they were back then for you. But the 'far better' is not as far better for us as it ought to be." You wanted to go to Africa, but you could not. Look out. One Man Garvey Movement, here I come!"

Never burn all of your bridges. Always give your job a two week notice before resigning. I was always resolved to that principle, and it never came back to haunt me.

But there seems to be one thing that haunts many Americans; we are so obsessed with an overwhelming sense of work ethic and patriotism, so answerable to the powers that be, that when we take a vacation, take a sick day or even resign from our jobs we actually feel a strong sense of guilt. For quite some time I kept getting this lingering impression that I was double crossing the system in America and abandoning it by going to Africa. It sort of reminds me of the slave that ran away under pressure and returned to the plantation under duress, but as I had said, I had no plans to return.

Before I knew it I was thirty three thousand feet in the air aboard the Alatalia bound for Rome, and from there to Africa and worlds unknown.

While flying over the Alps, there was nothing exciting, just the monotonous hum of the engine, restlessness of the passengers, and the glare of the snow below. But that is what a writer or an artist does. He takes a white or black blank page and puts his thoughts on it. As I gazed out of the port of the plane, between clouds and sky, I realized that I was drawing near to the very scenes where the drama of black history began. It was on those very Alps below that a Hammite of Carthage, Hannibal by name, pursued his raging quest to fulfill the vows placed on him by his father, Amlicar, when he was just nine years of age. Standing before the altar of Baal, he swore to carry out his father's quest to conquer Rome.

Hannibal took his Phoenician army, scores of footmen, and nine hundred elephants, after a great human loss in the freezing struggle. Hannibal audaciously stood at the gates of a terrified Rome. It was only later, in 202 BC, after bloody years of combat, that he was defeated on the battle fields of Zama. This marked the final blow to the Hammetic world empire. Never again would the black man as a race have his day in the sun. The sons of Japheth are now on the center stage of history. It is now their turn, and someday their Teutonic quest will crumble under the march of Moral Omnipotence.

When my story first began, the sons of Japheth were not faring so well in South Africa. There were the ghosts of Hess, Himmler, Goering, and Eichman, men whom the Second World War's Afrikaners were accomplices. Their ideologies continued through the seared conscience of John Vorster and Ian Smith as they gouged out the black man's visionary eyes of a better day.

Every stone was a potential grave marker. Every tree marked a burial. Freshly dug, unavenged graves filled the vastness of the land. It was in South Africa where the hoof beats of the black and gray horses of the apocalypse could be audibly heard day and night, thundering across the rusty tin covered shanties of Soweto. There, the ever grinning rotten skull of apartheid loomed over the black man's visionary head like a storm cloud, forever denying him the sweet privilege of a candid glance of a transcendental tomorrow.

It is a land where the sinister spirit of Hitler preaches racism from behind the gold studded pulpit of the Dutch

Reform Church. It is there for a hundred years that the bleached skeletons of innocent black men, women, and children were murdered by German Nazis. There they lay to this day in unceremonious burial, scattered across the desert floor like the Biblical dry bones in the valley.

All of this was done because there was a group of humans who had guns in their hands and under the inspiration of demons, felt that they had a God Given mission to destroy everyone whom they judged to be inferior to themselves. This was done in spite of the Divine ordinance that was proclaimed from the dawn of history that God hath made of one blood all nations of men to dwell on the face of the earth, and hath determined the times before appointed and the bounds of their habitation Acts. 17:26.

Where is the logic in what I am about to ask? And I truly apologize if I sound too derogatory. It is not my intention. Again, I ask, where is the logic when a man or a group of men become obsessed with a blind sense of arrogance, even to the extent that they have come to the notion that they are the only pure blooded humans put on earth by God

In other words, they have the audacity to lie down with a so called inferior receiver only to produce another inferior offspring that becomes the very image of his self. Where is the logic that says, "Since I can't afford to buy more slaves, I will procreate with my half human slave to produce more slaves and subject them to the same misery that their mother is subjected to?" Again I ask, where the logic that says, "My wife will never know nor will she ever notice or question that I started out with black skin slaves, but the new born ones look exactly like me?"

Somewhere back there logic took a leave of absence and had decided never to return.

Just below the Sahara, the black man was under nominal independence. He could not pry himself loose from the rigor mortis clutches of classical colonialism. For them, the milk of Mother Africa's once bulging breast has coagulated into the emphatic limpid of oblivious milklessness. Is this an abuse of poetic license? I think not. Neither is it is an abuse of the freedom of speech.

No truth is as naked as the infamous facts. On the other hand, it is not the truth that is naked. What is naked is the falsehood that has been exposed by the truth. For the most part, bias men have been the custodians of history. The further back that research allows, the more the bias. One has only to research Georges Cuvierin, the 1800s, and enquire into his disgusting exploits with the so called "Hotten tot Venus."

After long centuries of disgrace, it had to take the esteemed Nelson Mandela to give her body a decent burial.

My thoughts on the plane en route to Africa were overwhelming. The realities of actually traveling there were becoming more evident. The only home that I had was the plane I was on.

I began to consider the dark and sinister side of black history, "the black culprits."

To place the accounts of the races of human history on the opposite ends of a single scale would reveal that the atrocities of one side of the history of any race can never outweigh the discrepancies of another.

Therefore no history of any variation is complete without unveiling the entire truth about its dark side. There will always be those who are inspired to mimic the personification of evil.

With those thoughts in mind, I began to imagine various dark characters appearing alongside our plane. The first character was the human father of malevolence, a grandson of Ham. He was Nimrod of antiquity, King of Babel.

History testifies to his level of depravity. He was history's first bully, an outright blasphemer, history's Arc Totalitarian, an insatiable tyrant, worshipped as a god. Nimrod was the personification of apostasy. Even the fallen angels swore allegiance to him and he was their object of worship. He ravaged villages and build cities and towers.

The black Egyptians glorified Nimrod posthumously by erecting empire wide obelisk which actually memorialized his reported amputated penis. Centuries later, the Germans called obelisk their "iron fists." They used the obelisk as a standard. Today, the obelisk phallic stands sentinel at the Lincoln monument. Another stands in the Vatican's yard.

Nimrod's miter, (the head of the fish god, Dag) is officially worn by the Pontiff today.

Next appearing before me in the air, the black witch of black history. Her name was Jezebel, a Phoenician princess who became queen after marrying a Hebrew King. Her reign of terror was marked by her bathing in the blood of her enemies. She was a self-centered psychopath who had no rivals. Her unquenchable blood lust depicted her as an ancient "Bloody Mary." Her aggressiveness could be impaired only by an equally blood thirsty Hebrew archer, Jehu by name. Although Jezebel did not perish by Jehu's arrows as did her whimsical husband, she was never the less at the archer's command hurled from a tower by her disgusted eunuchs. Jezebel was partially eaten by starving dogs.

While speaking of dogs, I am reminded that the word for them is "canine," derived from Jezebel's ancestor Canaan, (meaning "low") son of Ham. Jezebel a Canaanite who worshipped a pantheon of gods. In addition to Baal, she also worshipped the "dog star," canis major. How blessed she must have been to have been gobbled up by the gods she loved,

What a smorgasbord of thoughts while sailing toward Europe. The very name of Europe itself is of Hammetic origin. The Greeks codified the mythology of Europa into their belief system. And to think that the "Baka" people whom we misnomerously labeled as "Pigmy" once inhabited what we now know as Europe.

This was three thousand years before the Teutonic arrived there to establish any credible history. The Baka dominated the land, flourished in trade, sailed the globe, warred with the Egyptians, and become the progenitors of the Madagascar nation. The proud history of the Baka should have never become a missing link in the annals of Black History.

The harvest of history will refuse to yield its richest treasures of knowledge to those who prejudice the original founders of its wisdom.

CHAPTER 4

DREAM SOIL

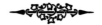

The twelve foot high fences on both sides of the walkway bulged with querulous onlookers as Avery and I were leaving the Cairo Airport to grab a taxi to enter the city. It was unimaginable how so many people could be up that early in the morning. We landed in Cairo between 1:30 and 2:00 a.m.

At last, there I was in Africa. As the old adage went, I was "a brother man in the Mother land" feet firmly on the sands of Egypt. Although it was sandy, it was Africa's sand. It was not exactly what I was looking for, but still Africa's sand, my dream sand.

Cairo was a bustling city named after the planet Mars. The place was teeming with people. All but I knew what they were saying. Undoubtedly there was bargaining, arguing, promoting their merchandise and of course everyone understands the universal language of laughter.

The youths, mostly boys, darted in and out of the busy bazaars. Many of the women had their faces covered. Some of them in polygamist families stayed close to each other as they trailed behind their husbands. The elderly sat about at ease, spending their leisure puffing hashish from extended tubes attached to a common vase. Other men were washing their feet in preparation for prayer. The mosque call to prayers rang out in distinct audible song and could be heard for miles. What a strange new world, where everybody seem to have the same agenda at least five times a day as they faced the east for prayer.

Streams of honking taxis drove frantically through the spit splattered streets as they selected lanes for driving convenience.

On the horizon, about fourteen miles distantance, loomed the Great pyramids. Their capstones peered down over the city from the top of a massive harmattan dust storm that had formed a wall that spanned the length of the Sahara. It was the dust from the desert that causes the chronic cough and spitting. If a man is as germ conscious as I am, he would actually do hop-scotch as he walked to prevent stepping in the spit that was splattered on the sidewalks. Every taxi driver seemed to have had the "Cairo hack," as I called it. Theirs was a constant cough and it was not in their custom to cover their mouths when they did. Of course, it was no different from quite a few people in America who practiced the same. In Egypt many drank from the same bottle, and ate simultaneously from the same bowl, so no doubt inhaling sprays from another man's cough probably would not add more germs to the ones that they already had. That is the way all over Africa.

It was quite obvious that Egypt would never become my home, and as anxious as I was to reach black Africa, I would not have forgiven myself if I had not taken the advantage of exploring one of the Seven Wonders of the World, the Pyramids.

There was an intense political unrest in the Egyptian air. A powder keg was about to explode. It was just a matter of time. It all seem to stem out of their President becoming too compromising with Israel. Nevertheless, I would take the chance of getting stuck in a country that could turn anti american overnight.

I had to see the Pyramids, I had to explore the Temples of Karnak, and in spite of my hurry to leave Egypt, I nevertheless had to experience how the pharaohs must have felt to be launched among crocodiles and sail the Nile to reach the Valley of the Kings. The risk was great. I was aware of the unstable political climate that fomented on the African continent as a whole. At any time a country's leader could be deposed. Many African countries were the puppets of foreign superpowers. The path to the African agenda was always clouded and obscured by outside imposing ideologies. There was always instability, always unrest, and more certain than ever, innocent blood would be shed.

Upon leaving Cairo, I glanced back at the city with a deep sigh, thoughts weighing heavy, realizing now after leaving the plane that my home was only where my two feet stood.

That parcel of land called Egypt, occupying Africa's eleven million six thousand square mile chunk of iron, ore, and uranium was at one time, many centuries ago, inhabited by the indigenous Cushite blacks.

The Bible called it the land of Cush and the land of Ham. Somewhere in the distant past, it appears that the inhabitants of Egypt (also known as Kemit, in antiquity) were forced on at least two occasions to abandon the land by invading warriors.

Although those events occurred centuries ago, no one could rightfully claim today that the contemporary Egyptians are squatters. It was just a passing thought that those early blacks of Egypt had to make a hasty exodus to where their descendants now reside in the lower Sudan, which was then Southern Egypt and further down into black Africa.

They were compelled to abandon the architectural genius of their ancestors. All takeovers are nasty. From the crusaders that invaded the Holy Land who boasted of how many Jewish babies they could hold on a sword to the exchange of bloodshed between the settlers and the North American natives, the time that the Roman Catholic Church landed in the Philippines, the slaughter of the Boxer Rebellion to Jan Smuts and his defeat at the Battle of Blood River. Blood mingled with blood, and when it does it is always indistinguishable as to whose blood it is.

I cherished my visit at Thebes more than I did the opportunity to see King Tut's sarcophagus. This was because Thebes was the burial place of the Pharaoh Queen, Hatshepsut. She was the foster mother of the great Biblical Moses.

In a way, it could be said that Africa is an extension of the Holy Land. She provided a temporary refuge for my Jewish Messiah, Yeshua. For the first two years of His earthly life, Mother Africa provided Him safety from His enemies. It was in Africa that Messiah learned to walk and talk. Only afterward would the Creator, His Father say to the ages, "Out of Egypt have I called My Son." Hosea 11:1. Matthew 2:15.

CHAPTER 5

THE RELUCTANT LAGGARD

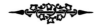

My determination to reach black Africa was over-whelming. I had wished that I could have seen more of Egypt but excitement was urging me on.

I had reached Africa after the colonial revolutions. Everyone was light headed. They were still celebrating their nominal detachment from colonial suzerainty and if but for a few years at least, they would bask in its light. Great charismatic leaders asserted themselves with rhetoric that fueled the masses. There was Jomo Kenyatta who warned his enemies that "The eagle in the air sees the chickens on the ground." There was Julius Nyerere's friendly reminder to his cabinet members that "When two elephants fight, it's the grass that suffers."

I was anxious to see these men and I could not allow myself to be detained by the glamour of Egypt. My quest there had been fulfilling, but still there was something missing. It was the human element, the warm fellowship, the comfort of company that Egypt could not provide for me.

The pyramids and temples could not give it. I would stare at the Sphinx and it only stared back at me in return. It had nothing to say, only the same loud silence and unbroken gaze that she had held for five thousand years. I needed humankind.

Avery and I finally parted. He told me that he was headed southward to Abu. From that day forward I never saw or heard from him again. Some Simbel years later, I had received the sad news that Avery had been murdered in America. I never learned how or why of his death, but I was deeply sadden by the news.

How indebted I was to Avery! That one night visit from him changed the course of my life. From the first time after my cousin and I split up, I felt a true loneliness. It was very different from the type of departure that one would have if he was in his own country. I felt stranded. Although I was surrounded by people, there I was with no one who spoke English. It too was an Islamic environment where I had gone, south into the Sudan.

A taxi driver, Mr. Mohammed, welcomed me into his home. He spoke no English but his kindness spoke for him. During most of my two weeks stay within his compound, I was alone. Mohammed was always out on the desert earning a living. His family kept me well fed and his children were very humble.

Mrs. Mohammed kept sending me food by her children. She too noticed my sadness. My biggest amusement there within their compound was watching the dung beetles roll goat balls across the desert floor, I had plenty of time to think and that I did. Where would I go from here? What will Africa do to me? Will she be as kind to me as Mr. Mohammed's family? Will she kill me? Will she make an exception of me and embrace me in her black arms, nurse me from her black breast or will she make an example of me and cast me out to her pet hyenas and lions? Would they devour my carcass or would I end up covered with maggots, as I would see so many times in my strolls through the bush? Would I sit with Kings, dine with Chiefs? Would Africa be a cruel Mother or a compassionate one?

All these questions would lie in wait as so many answers are never to be revealed at once. The future unveils one moment at a time. Hastiness may destroy the beautiful portrait of the future's design for our destiny. I kept hearing those immortal words: "Be careful for nothing, but in everything by prayer and supplication with thanksgiving let your supplication be made known unto God."

So the question arose. "Where would God take me? Would He destroy me or would He grant me mercy?" To His will I was resolved. Whatever lie ahead for me was undeniably real. The fantasies of America had passed. Nothing, absolutely nothing stood between my African brothers and me. There were no televisions, no space satellites controlled by selective media and no more divide and conquer propaganda. There stood the African and I, in our poverty and some times in his wealth. I was exposed to his customs, traditions, and all. Yes, I had it all including the sweltering sun, the stifling dust, and the red viscid mud, the filthy flies, deadly mosquitoes, torrential rains, soldier ants, black mambas, spitting cobras, fluttering butterflies, rotten human corpses, and myriads of fruit bats.

As repugnant as some of the things mentioned were, I was sold on the auction block of my own convictions, and Africa bought me not as a slave, but as a son returning home. The allure was even stronger than it was when I dreamed of her while walking the streets of America. It was as if l had gazed into Africa's "come hither" eyes,She winked and I was amorously compelled to surrender.

The heart of Africa seems to throb with a mixture of love and hate. There's a very strange phenomenon that seems to overwhelm those who come to Africa and remain there for some time. Men for centuries have come to the Dark Continent and fallen in love with her. Even after being mauled by lions and lived to tell about it, those who have been bludgeoned by tribes, bitten by snakes, drawn to death's door by deadly malaria, when they return to their comfortable homes in other parts of the world, they can find no rest until they have returned to Africa. Where ever they go, they carry Africa with them.

The intrigue and even the cruelty of the Black Mother cannot quell the insatiable thirst to nurse once again from her shriveling breast.

Africa brings to mind the life of another cousin to whom I was introduced in the very early years of my life. He was nearly my age. He loved his Mother with an undying passion, but she had no affection for him. She would nearly starve him and would often put him outside in the cold hallway of their ghetto apartment building until she had her fill of impassion lust with her lovers.

There sat my cousin quietly, often sobbing, waiting for the mother he loved so dearly to open the door, if only for a moment ,to enter for warmth and the comfort of seeing her face. But his mother was cold. The faint sound of his cry that entered her room from beneath the door, fell on deaf ears. But the callousness of his mother's heart never dimmed the flame that burned in his heart for her.

As the years took flight, and he became a man, he looked upon his aged mother, who by this time had become decrepit and deathly ill. Her lovers had long since gone, and most were dead. But she still had the love of her son. He lifted her feeble body up into his strong arms, carried her into his house, and looked after her well-being until she died.

He buried her in a notable cemetery and placed a tombstone upon her grave.

It read: "Here lies my Mother, whom I have always loved."

It can be said that Africa is in bed with her foreign lovers, but her survival will have to depend upon her own children who love her so passionately.

Like my wandering nomad counterparts in America, I traveling south, then west, crossing Africa by foot and fortitude.

CHAPTER 6

THE FRIEND

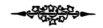

Ten months had gone by and my romantic intrigue with Africa had gone with it. The possibility of finding a job in the area where I was located was out of the question. I had to learn from bitter experience that when coming to Africa to stay, a person must either bring with him means of a livelihood, be sent to work by a substantial agency or come as an expatriate at the request of an African government. I had none of these. Had I gone perhaps to Liberia it would have been a different story. Black Americans are permitted to enter that country without a visa, and a job would have been easier to acquire.

The face in my mirror showed signs of stress. I actually felt myself aging. I was a septuagenarian before my time. Perhaps I exaggerate a bit, but mirrors don't lie. How much more of it could I take? I could not force myself to lie to others with a smile. I tried, but it just didn't work. I ask myself each day "What on earth was I thinking?"

I was now tasting the real Africa. How bitter it was. It

had gone from sweet to bitter sweet, from there to bitter again, and finally to actual wormwood. But I couldn't give up.

In Africa, a man can let go only when there is absolutely nothing more to cling to. He must hold on to any possible support that he has. It is like holding on to a rope suspended over a chasm. How will it end when it is no longer? If the rope snaps, or should his strength give way, he will die with a rigor mortis clutch to the rope and hold on, or grasp the wind in his fist until his corpse is skeletonized by scavengers, swinging there as a frightening reminder to by passers never to give up or to quit while you still have the time. The lessons of beauty and art are categorically unique and have much in life and morals to offer, but there are also lessons of wisdom that may be gained from the indelible imprints of the hideous and the grotesque, repelling though they may be. It is a picture of that ancient riddle of life that was put forth by the strongest man that ever lived "Out of the eater came forth meat, and out of the strong came forth sweetness."(Judges 14:14) reminiscent of a beautiful flower growing out of a dunghill.

It is a trembling thought to know that our deliberate failures in this world must be accounted for in the next. Moreover, it is not much more gratifying to know that the most rigid among our schoolmasters often produce the finest students although, they might graduate bearing the most crippling evidence of the lessons that they had to learn, they are none the less, the most notable among their alumni.

I was horrified by the despair of what I could become a

jobless vagabond, a drifter, a repugnant interloper, a recipient of the scraps of Africa's tender hearted mothers or just picking through the market garbage heaps and squabbling over salvaged filth. At best, I could see nothing before me but the worse. Only I was the author of the blank pages of my miserable future, as many of us are.

Often it happens at the very moment that we can see before us nothing but hopeless quagmires of dark promises that the God of heaven intervenes. It is as if He is testing us to see what we will do with a single ray of light. I did, of course, what any man in a dungeon would do with it. I would follow its path and stay with its journey across the room. I would then thank God at the end of the day for its gleam of grace.

Had it not been for that ray of hope, my desponded soul, like some stranded ship, would have been cast upon those treacherous shoals and driven back upon the jagged reefs of madness. It was all too surreal, too super sobering for a man like myself who had not that long ago come from a fantasy world like America. It were as though I was standing on an island that was small enough only for my two feet as I helplessly counted the minutes when that mounting tide would embrace me in its briny bosom and sink me to the bottom of nothing.

There was nothing particularly inviting about that morning either as I walked down the steps of an acquaintance's porch. I was cheered on by a symphony of frogs that surrounded the compound. Their incessant warbling was in fact a blend of pure music so loud that they were and deafening, but refreshing.

I soon strolled on to the red dirt road that led to the lively town of Victoria, Cameroon in West Africa. Over the months, I had gotten into the habit of kicking over coconut shells as I walked. Those shells contained stagnant rain water and incubated mosquito larvae. It brought me a little relief to think that for every shell turned over, a life was being saved. In fact, I had gotten pretty good at it and was thinking seriously about organizing a "Shell Kicking Club" with incentives. The chorus of frogs eventually gave way to the most astounding sound of school girls singing.

There they were, headed in my direction, all dressed in blue. What a beautiful song a Christian hymn their melodious voices were blended in perfect harmony. The girls were as beautiful as the song they sang. Practically all of them were indigo. Everybody on the road was compelled by the sweetness of their anointed voices. They had captured us all and we could do nothing but to stop and gaze. The frogs had even stopped to listen. I watched them until they turned a bend in the road and were out of sight.

Even then, I stood listening as I strained to hear the faintest sound of their angelic voices, so enrapturing, for those few minutes, I had completely forgotten about the battle that I was having. I learned later they were students of the Alfred Saker Girl'Beauty is still in the earth. I thought and nothing, absolutely nothing can destroy it"

Whenever outward beauty is marred, inward beauty will surface. Those who love beauty will someday soon bathe in its efulgence.

As one man has so eloquently stated, "There to quaff

the pleasures of life from the foaming goblet of the Infinite," and I must add, Those who do not believe it, will never have the pleasure of ever seeing it."

Suddenly, I was approached by a maroon Peugeot, which drove in front of me. The driver pulled over to the side of the road and stopped. As I came closer, I recognized the driver. He had driven past me several times before in the past, not failing to greet me by tapping his horn. This time he spoke out in Pidgin English.

"Which side una de go?"

I had no idea of what he was saying, so I simply responded. "Good morning, Brother, I didn't quite get you."

He wore a smile. "Oh, sorry," he replied. "I see you're not quite familiar with our Pidgin English, eh?"

"I'm trying to learn it," I replied. "I think that it's really cool—unique, in fact."

"May I give you a lift?" he asked.

"Oh, that would be great, thanks," I answered.

As my Samaritan began driving, he gave me a curious glance out of the corner of his eye.

"The name's Tabby, and yours?"

"Tyler Holiday. Just call me Holiday."

"Ah, an American, I see, a black American, Welcome to our country. I believe they call you a Negro, is zat so?" It was just a simple question, no sarcasm.

"Yes, that's what we are often called."

Tabby enquired further. "Well, if you don't mind my asking, and of course no offense, where does the word nigga fit in?"

"Well Mr. Tabby, I laughed as I began. "Your guess is almost as good as mine, but let's just say that the name was first applied to the black people of America by a people of brighter skin color who felt that the name was, for some reason, suitable. Black men who were brought there had their own names from the tribes where they came from. You know, Yorba, Ebo, Bamenda, et cetera. No one cared anything about the delicate ethnic divisions among the black people. So I just suppose that a 'bunch of niggers' was the easiest way out. Some of our own blacks adopted it and decided to apply it to other blacks. Sometimes we do it in anger. Some times in jest, Even the white man has demeaning names for men of his color."

Tabby was taking it all in.

"Do you know what our children call white people who come here to our country?" he asked.

"No, I have no idea...What?"

"The peeled ones," he said. "They call them the peeled ones. You know, like what a potato looks like after you have peeled it?" He laughed as if he was tickled by the thought.

"Well, Tabby, I said, "I am glad that God has decided for me that I should be the complexion that He has decreed for me. And now I know for certain there are only two things that I must do."

"What are those?" Tabby asked.

"Stay black and die."

Tabby looked at me for a second and suddenly burst out in laughter. "My, my!" he said. "You have a sense of humor."

"On the other hand," I added, "I am a blend of

African with a Black Foot Indian Patent. So I straddle two continents."

"Tell me, my friend. What brings you here to our beautiful country?"

"Returning home, I suppose you could say."

Tabby spoke again, "But tell me, my friend, you seem a bit worried."

Even he could tell my face must have spoken volumes. Tabby reduced his speed as I answered. "Well, I do have a concern. I need a job desperately."

Tabby responded, "Looking for a job, huh?...but our country is so small and backward. Why should you leave the comforts of your advanced America, to come here and suffer with us?"

That was the very question that I had been asking myself.

As I adjusted my sitting position to face Tabby, the answer came.

"Have you ever heard of the "Negro National Anthem?""

"No," Tabby responded slowly. "I can't say that I have."

"Well," I replied. "It is a very beautiful and touching song. It was written by James Weldon Johnson. At the very end of the last stanza the words sing, "Shadowed beneath thy hand, we may forever stand, true to our God, true to our Native land."

"How beautiful,!" Tabby said, nearly breathless. "How beautiful!"

"Well," I continued, "It is in that song that we are singing about our Mother Africa, our native land. There was a time in our history that we blacks in America had pledged to be true to Africa, but somewhere along the line broke that solemn pledge...and, I might add, that we blacks as a whole, have not been true to our God as well.

"If we have broken that pledge, then it stands to reason that no other commitment is worth keeping. God first, country second."

I initiated a change in our conversation. I spoke somewhat incognito. That is, as if I wasn't already aware of it, I reminded Tabby that he had mentioned something to me about "suffering."

"Come, come, Holiday, you can't tell me that you haven't noticed. Just look about you. We have nothing here. No factories, at least not to amount to anything. Let me tell you a little story." Tabby began by unfolding a sad chapter to his country's history.

"It was years ago, when the cruel Germans were forced to pull out of our country, all that they left behind was their language, some buildings and Kaiser Wilhelm's castle in the mountains.

"The Germans did not teach our elders to speak their language. They forced them to learn it. Our people despised the Germans. A few of our warriors got some small revenge by ambushing a few Nazi soldiers and cutting out their gums and teeth. After drying them out, they fastened them to their calabashes.

"Our warriors did not have guns at the time. They used only their machetes."

It was later during my stay in Africa that a photographer

confided in me and gave me a picture of some very old men, displaying some teeth attached to their drinking gourds as they stood holding machetes.

Tabby continued his story.

"Finally, after the Germans pulled out for good. We found ourselves under British control. The British left us with a miserable dependence. To this day, we rely on them for everything. Only a privileged few are enjoying even that. We call that 'Neo-Colonialism.'

"The Europeans operate our coca plantations, but we depend upon what we call 'the extended family unit'. Without it, we are finished."

"Actually, it's the women who are the back bone of Africa. They find food. They raise the children. It is they who carry the heavy loads on their heads and backs."

As Tabby was discussing African women, we noticed one woman who was on the side of the road. She supported a sack of something on her head. It must have weighed fifty pounds or more. She had a baby tied to her back and she also carried a large basket in her hand. But her stride was graceful. She walked with as much grace as a fashion model.

"What of your black women in America, sah? They must also be as powerful as well, eh?"

"Yes indeed, they are." I answered. "They are the glue of the family. Beautiful, strong, and strong willed. We men in America can learn much from our women. But what about your government?" I asked. "What are they doing with the revenue given to them by other countries?"

"The government?" came the reply. "Please, sah, don't

make me laugh. What a joke," Tabby continued soberly.

"Now don't get me wrong, my friend. Our law, that is our Constitution in this country is a fairly good one, I'd say... but it's some of the people at the top, such as the cabinet ministers, the Governor, the Office of the Attorney General and the members of Parliament. Some of those guys were elected from right out of the bush country. Many of them can barely read or write. I see them as the ones that are manipulated by the educated politicians, you know. They are made to feel more important than they really are and told that they are far better than their own people.

"Once in a while a clever person emerges from the bush country. He is mistakenly invited into the Parliament and he becomes a power to be reckoned with. At any given chance, he will act in his own interest. Those are recipes for disaster because that is how "coups " are are started."

Tabby stopped talking long enough to catch his breath. I could see the frustration on his face. Apparently, politics was his line of interest.

"Do you mind if I stop for a minute, friend?" He asked.

"Not at all!" I said. He braced himself before proceeding.

"Take for example, we have in our country, palm oil from the plantations, coffee, rubber, aluminum and even oil rigs, but the masses see no benefits from the proceeds. My God, man let's face it! this stuff is exported out of this country by the billions."

"Perhaps it's protection money against bully nations," I added.

"Whatever it is, the people see nothing of it." he said.

"Most of the Ministers are arrogant bastards driving around in their Mercedes Benz, looking down at their noses at every one. They pocket the money and use it for their personal affairs. They send their children to Europe and America for an education, praying that they will return and step into their shoes. In the meantime, the rest of the nation can go to hell in a hand basket."

Tabby's resentment had gained momentum. Quite obviously, he had waited a long time to vent. Strangers sometimes make good counselors, especially if they are willing to listen. He went on to explain how the people in his area were nothing more than soccer balls that is, as far as their government was concern. The gross ill treatment of human beings was outrageous and uncalled for.

"We are kicked around by the local authorities here." he said. "They are like spontaneous totalitarians. Should they suspect that there is the slightest political unrest among us, they will not hesitate to come down on us with their gendarmes. They come in with their canes, clubs, and hippo tails, bludgeoning any person that they see on the road."

One sad story that Tabby told me was almost unbelievable.

"A very dear friend of mine and his wife," he said, "were walking along this very road. They were both picked up by the police and driven back to the station. He was accused of trying to overthrow the government, which, of course, was not true. He was merely protesting the poor treatment of employees by the powers that be.

"My friend was tortured, and beaten, nearly losing an

eye. His wife was stripped of her clothes, douched with water and had electric pinchers attached to her breast. This went on for hours until she couldn't take it any longer. She died right there inside the station. The worst part about it, was that nothing, absolutely nothing was ever done about it,"

Tabby's eyes began to trickle. He also cautioned me to be sure to have identification on at all times.

"It is mandatory that we citizens carry an ID that says 'One Man, One Vote' on it. We do not have Democrats and Republicans here. We don't even have a democracy."

Tabby ended his frustrations after telling another horrifying tale that had recently occurred. It involved the most unbelievable act of treachery.

"Even our politicians operate within a vicious circle. Always stabbing each other in the back."

This time, Tabby raised his car window up, making sure that his words wouldn't escape. There were some pedestrians that had walked too close to his car and seemed to be eavesdropping. It was a typical African past time.

"Why, it was just a few weeks ago that one of our very fine politicians a relative of mine, in fact died a most horrible death. He was a member of the cabinet. He arrived home one evening, tired, ate dinner, took a shower and climbed into bed. After switching off his lamp, he felt this cold, elongated piece of slippery flesh unfolding alongside his body. He frantically threw back his sheet, switched on the lamp, only to find this six foot King Cobra staring right into his face."

The very thought of this made me jittery, I was also horrified to realize that this occurred right here in the very area where he resided.

I later watched a cobra of enormous length swimming along a stream. It was headed in the direction of a group of woman who were in that same water, washing their clothes. At the same time, there were some people yelling at them from the top of an embankment to get out of the water.

Tabby continued.

"I am not kidding you, Holiday," he said. "It was a blow to our entire family. Now let me finish telling you about this. My relative let out this loud scream as he scrambled for the door. About that time, the cobra lunged out and planted it's venomous dripping fangs right smack on his buttocks. Now the poor bastard was running about in his compound, terrified, screaming and kicking in his wives' doors. They think that he had suddenly become possessed with demons. So while they were trying to get away from him, he was trying to get them to suck the venom out of his katukas.

"His mother-in-law refused. His very own grandmother suspected that he had been bewitched, so she too felt that it would be too disrespectful to do such a thing. So the poor son of gun just died. Believe me, brother. This was in the newspapers just a few days ago. It was a suspected assassination. Many of our people suspect the Donel Family of having one of our country men to do their dirty work."

I stared in shock at what I had just heard.

"Who are the Donel Family?" I asked.

"Yes, yes they are a very wealthy French aristocratic

family that our government contracted out to take over our electrical system. My cousin who died had recently opposed the inhumane treatment of the black employees by the Donels. They work them like dogs, paying them very low wages and or barely paying them at all. The blacks were so incensed by this outrage that they went on a strike. When my cousin confronted the Donels...well, that was when he was killed.

"Some of our other politicians accepted a bribe from the Donels, so new people were hired to replace the ones which were fired. Those who were terminated were never compensated or given back pay. To accept bribes in such a small country as ours is a sellout to everybody. In fact, it is an act of treason."

Tabby started up his car again, this time driving at walking pace. The conversation changed. He spoke up. "So, you really need a job, eh?"

"Oh, you can't imagine how badly," I exclaimed.

"Well, what was your job in the states?"

"I worked with law enforcement in the military for a while. I taught a bit in a seminary, I also...."

Tabby interrupted.

"Teaching? Teaching what?" Tabby showed renewed excitement.

"Comparative Religion, New Testament Greek and although I am not very good at it, my heart is with Biblical Hebrew."

"Then that means that you can also teach English as a second language, eh, Holiday?"

"Sure can" I answered.

"My, oh my," Tabby shouted. "I could kick myself. Why did I not think of him before? What is going on with me?" he explained.

"Think of who, before, Tabby?"

"Well, I know a man that is, a Chief, Chief Omubu. He is the Proprietor of the Secondary School down in Kamba. It is quite a distance from here, but let me ask you, Holiday, did you bring your particulars along with you?"

"Particulars?"

"Yes, you know, your degrees, any certificates, and so forth."

"Oh yes, yes, of course,"

"Good, then," Tabby answered. "There should be no worry…uh, of course you've already tried our Government, I suppose?"

"Yes, but…."

"I know, I know," he said. "Those bastards are slower than honey can flow in the South Pole, and besides, they would only demand a bribe from you if they saw how anxious you were. In addition to that, you would have to spend half of your tour of duty proving to them that you are not a spy. Small countries are always suspicious, yet it is the exploiters who are running the country. Who needs spies when you have exploiters?"

"Uh, tell me about it." I answered. "America invites spies from other countries in every day, and it's difficult for me to believe that they are not aware of it."

Tabby began muttering, changing the conversation.

"His name is Chief Victor Omobu" "What a character he is!"

"Who are we talking about?" I asked.

"Chief Omubu, he is the Proprietor of the Rodgers Faircourt Secondary School, often called a college. It's about two hundred miles from here, a few miles from Kamba Town. It's far out into the bush."

I could hardly believe my ears.

"You mean to say that he is a real African Chief?!"

"Oh yes" Tabby answered. "He is by all means, a real Chief. I've known him for some years, but it's been many years since I have seen him. He was in a sour mood when I last saw him.

"The Chief and I were together some time ago in the National Assembly. He represented one small province and I represented another." Tabby began to chuckle. "The Chief became very bitter when they kicked him out of the Parliament. He did not have much representation within the government, but he still has powerful friends up there... But it was far more to it than that."

Tabby began to lower his voice. Although he and I were still inside of his car, it just made for extra caution. "The Chief left out of the assembly a very angry man. He was in something of a disgrace. He promised to put a thousand curses on every one of them.

"Of course, some of them ignored his threats but others took them quite seriously. You see, most Africans take witch-craft very seriously. Even our Presidents have their personal witches and witch doctors. Before they take a trip abroad to discuss international affairs with your President or with any head of state, for that matter they always consult their witches first. Take Idi Amin for example he murdered many innocent people just on the whim of his witch's counsel."

"Yes" I answered, "Even some American Presidents and their wives have been known to consult their spiritual advisors such as trans-channelers and séances" "Sorry for my interrupting you. As you were saying about the Chief?"

Tabby continued, "Yes, yes, well, you see, the Chief became suspect when the mishandling of some funds were discovered. It was a tremendous amount of money. The evidence pointed to the Chief but the Authorities could not prove it. It was a known fact that the Chief lived a lavish life style. He was quite fond of the women, wine and food. He had plenty of those things. During the investigation, the authorities interrogated the Chief so severely that when it was over, he stood outside on the Parliament steps and cursed them to the high heavens. There was one thing that he was heard saying that was so staggering, so unabashed, that as a matter of fact, it would take either a mad man or somebody with an extra pair of testicles to stand where he was standing and to say what he was saying. He was heard to say, "So you think that I am a swine that would gobble up your money eh? Well, I will show you what a swine can do, you bastards, I am not afraid of you, any of you!"

"The Parliament members assumed that anyone having the guts to make such a public display had to be either a total fool or completely out of his mind. Since we don't prosecute the insane in our country, the Chief's threatening insinuations were ignored. The Chief was not to be under-estimated. Either his performance on the Parliament steps that day was on purpose to make them think that he had gone mad, or he intended for them to take his promises for what they intended them to be.

"Considering the fact that the Chief at this time was being escorted out of the Parliament hall by two gendarmes under his arms, he actually tore his self from their gasp when he went into this outrage."

"So the officials just backed away from the Chief?" I asked.

"Oh yes." Tabby answered. "The Parliament failed to realize that even the bush country may produce individuals that may be reckoned with. Rumor has it that the Chief had actually acquired enough money to start up a Secondary School. He was clever enough not to name the school after his self, so he wouldn't draw suspicion. He then contacted a British Philanthropist whom he had met while in Parliament. This gentleman gave a handsome contribution toward the Chief's enterprise. The school was given his name, 'Rogers Faircourt.'

I tell you Holiday, the man is finished in government."

Curious to know a little more, I asked, "So, are you still affiliated in any way with the National Assembly?"

A sadness shaded his face. "No, not anymore. " He answered. "Those were the golden days. There's a lot that I haven't told you about myself, but it is not me that matters, it's you. You, my brother, should be off to see the Chief."

I expressed a little nervousness.

"But after what you have described to me about the Chief...I"

Tabby placed his hand on my shoulder and said, "Don't worry, don't worry, No harm will come to you. I must admit that if there was another place that I could recommend you, believe me, I wouldn't hesitate to do so. But please, give it a try. I'm sure that after you talk to the Chief, he will hire you. Wait, I will do even better. I will introduce you to him by letter. He will remember me."

At that moment, for the first time since being in Africa, I felt that I was beginning to belong. A weight had seemingly fallen from my shoulders.

I asked myself, "Are my troubles really over?" The answer returned, "Now, Holiday, hasn't life taught you by now that no one's troubles are ever really over? The struggles against trouble end only at death, provided that you have made peace with God through the death of His Sacrificial Son Yeshua."

I thanked Tabby for his help. He simply said, "Oh, think nothing of it. It was a pleasure to make your acquaintance. It is I who should thank you for lending me an 'ear of burden.' By the way, keep those things to yourself that we have discussed, okay? I'll drop by your place tomorrow with the letter."

"You have my word, Tabby" I assured him as we shook on it.

CHAPTER 7

ON TO KAMBA

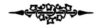

As I was getting out of Tabby's car, he caught me by the arm.

"Just a minute," he said as he reached into his shirt pocket, pulling out a roll of money.

"Take this. It'll carry you to Kamba and help you after you have reached there."

I teared up.

"But, Tabby, you've already done enough. I just couldn't …"

"Go on, Take it. Don't be silly " he insisted as he pushed my hand away, then added, "One can never do enough for one's brother. This world is round. One good deed always deserves another. You will always do good to others when you have been encouraged by those who have done good to you. At least that's what my father always said."

To this day I remember Tabby. He was such a kind man, a perfect stranger, heaven sent, a man who had accepted my dilemma as his own.

Although, like my cousin Avery, I never saw Tabby again, I believe that he was among the servants of heaven that are often sent by your side to assist, and when their task is complete, they just vanish away.

After receiving Tabby's letter that Sunday evening, which he had sent to me by the hand of a small boy, I had decided to leave for Kamba the following day.

It was about four thirty in the morning when I reached the Victoria Motor Parking Lot. It was already crowded with anxious travelers and the place was lively.

There was music all around and squawking parrots overhead, cutting the air making their way across the azure sky. It was a typical west African scene, with extremely tall palm trees reaching up to drink the first glimmer of sun light. Babies, up too early exposed to the coolness of the morning, protested with loud cries. A few potbellied tots with their protruding navels joined in the concert. There were obstinate goats being lead about, pigs squealing with tight cords tied around their legs and necks, and caged chickens cackling. Among other things, I saw something that I never would have imagined.

There was a man holding a cage containing two very small animals. One was a chimpanzee, the other a baboon. Both seemed frightened their eyes stretching. The baboon being younger, clung tightly to his partner which seem to accept it with parental embrace.

Children ran about the lot selling homemade bread, boiled eggs, dried fish, pineapples and delicious smelling roasted sawyer on sticks. Chew sticks were available and were used as tooth brushes. They shouted loudly, "Buy my own! Buy my own! Please sah!, Please sah!"

The taxi drivers were by far the most entertaining. They were literally snatching passenger's luggage and bundles out of their hands. It all appeared to be just a rough, unscrupulous game of lolly gagging, a combination of wrestling and a tug-o-war with other people's personal property. Sleepy passengers had no choice but to come to life as they chased the drivers across the lot in order to keep up with their belongings. You couldn't help but laugh.

Now and then a playful passenger being in the same jovial mood would shout, "Hand me back my luggage, you fool. You going to delay me my journey,"

The drivers often solicited their destinations in loud, audible pidgin English "Doula dey? Any one for Doula?"

"Buea dey-dey?"

"Some mon dey fa Eknoa?"

"Who dey fa Mutengene?"

"Mumfe!, Mumfe!, Mumfe!?"

"Anyone dey Bamenda?"

"Benda deah?"

Finally, my ride rang out, three sharp shouts, "Kamba, Kamba, Kamba!"

In excitement, I responded, "Which taxi fa Kamba?"

An eager lad assisted me, pointing out my taxi, "Dat moto de-ah, sah, dat one be na fa Kamba. De one whiti dey callum, Sista."

Sister was written in bold letters on the side of a faded maroon Peugeot jalopy.

I spotted it parked just on the other side of an extended three foot wide mud puddle. The only way to cross it was to jump. If you should jump short of the other side, to your fate was a face or feet full of the filthiest gook of hepatitis that one could ever wish for.

On the other side of the mud pie stood the proud driver of the Sister. He had the biggest smile on his face, showing all three of his teeth. From his smile, it was hard for me to determine whether he was wishing that I would clear the mud or splash in it. Perhaps the guy was indifferent. Maybe it was just me being a little paranoid. In either case, it made no difference. I had to get to Kamba. There I stood before the "Puddle of Challenge" with my luggage in my hands. I took four big steps backwards. I was going to clear that sucker come hell or high water. Then I envisioned the horror of myself missing the other side in safety. I saw "hep" bugs all over me, taking over my miserable frame, consuming my very fiber until at last I had become one with the elements, a brother to the arrogant worms that would look sneeringly down upon me as they joined in laughter with the driver of the Sister.

The Sister was already taking on passengers. I had to jump this puddle. "To hell with it all Sister, here I come!"

I made an attempt to run but had to come to a halt when an elderly man cleared the puddle with the most astounding agility. About that time, an old woman no doubt, his wife swished past me, and she too would have won a gold medal in the Olympic broad jump.

Age in Africa is just what it is, age. It has nothing to do

with performance. Performance is eternal in Africa. If you aren't dead, then you can jump. After a pregnant woman tried the puddle and succeeded, I began to feel quite stupid. So there I was. I took a double grip on the handles of my luggage, got on my mark, and was about to take my great leap forward when suddenly, to my astonishment, I found myself struggling with two drivers who had rushed over to me and grabbed my luggage. They were contesting for my services and there I was in the middle of that same old tug-o-war.

The drivers said nothing to me but bickered back and forth.

"Release dis bag!giffum, giffum!"

A crowd was gathering around. The two continued, "Dis customa be na my own, I don seen him fust!"

The other man spoke out, "Unhand dees bags, you bush man!"

The other, "You be na de bush man, you mimbo eye!"

It was later that I learned that there was a wine called Mimbo. A person with mimbo eyes were like wine.

This bickering had to stop. I had to jump this puddle, get into the Sister and leave Victoria. I raised my voice, "Hey! Hey! Let go my luggage!"

The men politely backed away and there I was, facing the mud. With a running start, I cleared that puddle like a pro, got into the taxi with the other passengers, and off to Kamba we went.

The ride was miserable. African drivers speed like demons. The more trips they can make, the more money they make. The rate of speed at which they travel, absorbs all of a passenger's attention.

At one point while we were reaching the likelihood of potentially having our wretched bodies thrown from the car and scattered in every possible direction and some of our unforgiving souls in another, a rooster added to our nightmares by darting out into the road directly in front of us. Our driver made a sudden effort to keep from hitting it by swerving to the opposite side of the road.

His turn was so sharp that our taxi was running on two wheels. I was sitting directly behind him and all I could see was red dirt road. As we nearly turned over, passengers were screaming hysterically. I was in the lead. It was at that moment that my life flashed before me. Instinctively, we all tried as desperately as we could to lean to our right in an effort to straighten the wheels. Thank God it worked. The taxi was filled with groans.

Those caged monkeys that I saw back at the parking lot were also tied down in the back of the taxi. Their shrill screams were deafening. Both man and monkey had joined in panic. Perhaps the monkey's lives flashed before them as well. Let me guess. They no doubt saw nothing but bananas, baboon butt and boiled eggs.

As soon as we were squarely back on all fours, the passenger's tempers flared. The things that came out of their mouths were unbelievable. The first reaction was from a man sitting next to the driver. He gave the driver a hard, solid punch and shouted, "What de hell man!? You idiot. You go take my life for sake of fowl?"

Hearts were pounding. Mine in the lead. If there was ever a time that Africa didn't need drums, that was the time.

Another shouted, "Who de hell taught you how to drive, a bush doctor!?"

The driver retorted, "Who is driving dis taxi, me or you?"

A passenger answered, "I tell you man, you may be driving dis damn ting, but I didn't pay you to drive me to hell!"

Another passenger, somewhat intoxicated, commented as he glanced back at the monkeys, "And just to tink, I would have some tall explaining to do if I had arrived at de pearly gates with a dam baboon clinging to my blok ass and holding a chimpanzee by de hand."

Finally, an elderly man turned to me. He was trembling frantically as he spoke to me. "Young man, I don't know your name."

"It's Holiday" I answered nervously.

"Well, Holiday, should we ever meet again, passing on de road, please do for me a very big favor."

"And what would that be sir?" I asked, still shook up.

"Please, please remind me neva to ride with dis bastard again. As a matter of fact, I am on my way to attend a burial, but I certainly had not planned it being my very own."

He had spoken loud enough for the driver to hear, but the driver gave no response.

That was a harrowing experience. I had promised myself from that very day that somehow, someway, if I continued to stay in Africa, I would buy my own car. If destiny had it that I would have to exit this world by car, then I would rather it be by my own hand and not by somebody else's.

CHAPTER 8

ENANGA

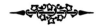

As soon as we stepped out of the taxi, we were surrounded by several dozen screaming, potbellied children. Most of them were partially dressed. Others were naked. All of them were cheerful, on a mission for their parents, soliciting their fruits, boiled eggs and loaves of bread. Some asked for money.

There was one child that caught my attention, although my heart went out to all of them. She was a three year old girl, so tiny and so fragile that it was all she could do to stand up against the on rush of the bigger children. Her faint voice was nearly drowned out by the anxious competitors. She came up to me holding a boiled egg in her hand.

The little girl's dress was tattered, soiled, and torn from one of her shoulders. It was difficult for me to tell whether she was happy or sad, but she was truly a beautiful child. She looked up into my face. Her skin was nearly jet. Tiny sweat beads sparkled on her ultricious hairline. Her cute little nose was smeared with glassy mucus. I reached down and cupped her almond shaped face and spoke in what little Pidgin English I knew, asking her name.

"Your nam na whiti?"

While sniffing her nose, she answered back so seriously, "Ma nam na Enanga."

I bought her egg and placed a couple of extra coins in her tiny little hands. She skipped away with a broad smile to tell her parents.

For some reason, I could never forget her name: "Enanga."

Through all these years it stuck with me, all though I never learned its meaning. It was so original, so fitting.

That precious little Enanga was a significant one of the significant millions of Africa's children who may speak out one day and call to the world's remembrance that in spite of the caring minority, in Europe and in the West, the rest of the masses remained callous and indifferent. Africa's youth will say, "Our Face Books and You Tubes have shown us that while you sat in the comfort of your living rooms, and saw our emaciated faces, did that not move you to tears? Was it not compelling enough to cause you to lose your appetite? It was I whom you saw lying with a skeletal frame in the sweltering heat while I was begging you with silent breath to rush to my side. There I was before you in full color. Why did it not shake your foundation when I stared into your dry eyes with my sunken ones? It was I that you glanced at with indifference before you turned the page and reached for another sandwich. You wanted only my gold and my diamonds, but you consigned me to a far worse hell than the one that I was already in."

Yes, Enanga will remember.

By that time, she may be Mother Enanga, Doctor Enanga, Princess Enanga, or perhaps President Enanga, but she will remember the apathy of the corporate, lusting west.

It was some years later that I sat with a woman in Africa for seven hours at an outpost bus stop. We watched her twelve year old son as he lay dying in his mother's arms. The child had dwindled to the size of a six year old. His exhausted mother, famished and drained of her strength, had carried the child on her back for over a distance of twenty miles. She had walked from the interior of the bush country.

She and I were headed in two separate directions, she to the hospital and I to the big city. There we had to wait at the same bus stop. After a few hours we saw an approaching land rover occupied by some Europeans. They were headed in the direction of the hospital. Since the woman didn't speak English, I spoke up for her.

"She needs help desperately. Her son is dying hospital, please!"

The three of them looked at the woman and waved their hands exclaiming, "No time. No time," and with those words they sped off leaving a stifling cloud of dust in our faces. The child died a couple of hours later.

The wailing mother tied the limp body of her beloved son to her back then again started her long journey back to her village. The last thing that I recalled was seeing her accompanied by thousands of flies, which had already been attracted by the stench of decay.

How precious are the little ones around the world. Today they are in our hands. Tomorrow we will be in theirs. I pray that they will not become our future threat and they will, if we allow, our love for them to speak louder than the truth against our exploitation of them. Oh the dangers of promiscuity!. If we fail to provide for them only the essentials needed, we will do them a damming disfavor. They will be indistinguishable from many nation's youths that are being nourished on sacred lies and must perpetually experience a renascence of blood in a futile effort to gain a temporary peace.

It is only righteousness that exalts a nation, but sin is a reproach to any people.

That righteousness must derive from absolute truth.

Our children are our present reminders of the lessons that we have long forgotten. We, like Enanga, were once innocent, simple, dependent, and even helpless and are we still not helpless? Are we not at the mercy of the staggering powers that rotate by the trillions above our heads? Are we not at the mercy of a galaxy whirling compassionate Father who longs in His heart for us to call him "Daddy?"

The youth of Africa may yet provide for us the answers that we have sought for centuries. That same genius that gave the world the pyramids and the Zimbabwe ruins may still be lying dormant, asleep in the wound of Mother Africa where it was once conceived, and now the sons and daughters of that genius may be waiting for the right era, the exact moment to be born anew. Perhaps someone in some forgotten tribe of Africa may now be holding in his hand the very remedy for the eradication of that deadly disease that has plagued our planet for so long.

The blinding sun caused me to squint as I tried to get another look at my surroundings. The dazzling glitter on the aluminum roofs of the market booths reflected brilliantly. A hand over my eyes served little purpose. Shimmering mirages danced on the ground ahead.

CHAPTER 9

THE SCHOOL

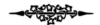

A few cart pushers that would have normally fallen over the top of each other to earn courtesy fees for carrying luggage showed no effort to abandon the comfort of their shade. Who could blame them? It was much hotter in this area than it was back in Victoria. The very act of begging kept those with leprosy on the alert. They had no choice. For them it was beg or die. Although the majority of the market population appeared to be listless, none of them were to be taken for granted. It would be an erring assumption on the part of any one to under estimate the African's innate alertness. There is never a time when you are not being watched, watched like a hawk. A fellow African can recall to you six months from the day exactly where you were, what you were wearing, who it was that you were talking to, and word for word what your conversation was about. Most of the time he will comment on the character of the person that you were befriending. Not only that, but he will not hesitate to caution you against any one whom he thinks may be an unwary person. He will further remind you that "association begets assimilation."

This is also a Biblical warning, "Evil communications corrupts good manners." 1 Corinthians 15:33.

In Africa someone is always listening in. That is another reason why one should never talk African politics. A person's open disapproval against an African President may prompt an early official knock at his door. That can be quite costly. It may land him in jail or earn him a swift deportation, if not his very life. Of course in the land of the free and the home of the brave, curses and dehumanizing are religiously heaped upon the President. If those demeaning invectives were tangibly weighed, they would not only tilt the scale against the national deficit, but would catapult it into orbit. It is so far removed from those who asked George Washington to be their king.

In Africa, a President Elect is King,

I spotted a man leaving the market and caught up with him. "Excuse me please," I called out. He turned with a smile, a bit startled.

I continued, "Could you kindly direct me to the home of Chief Omubu?"

"Schua, schua," returned the strong accent. "I also be passing dat wey. We wak togeda."

There was momentary silence between us.

Finally I asked, "Is it always as hot as it is today?"

The man laughed. "Oh yes, yes sometimes even hotta! We Africans are much use to it...but den sometimes it can git very cold, especially during middle of da yeah. It tis at dat time dat all we have is rain and mud."

After walking for about a half a mile, heat bearing down, I began to feel dizzy. "Hold on," I said, trembling. "I've got to sit down...thirsty" The man understood. He agreed.

After about ten minutes we started our journey. It wasn't long before we turned on to a narrow road and then came, "There's da Chief's house," and before I could thank him, he exclaimed, "It was nice meeting you sah." and off he went.

Still exhausted, I approached the house, then paused to fumble for Tabby's letter. The Chief's house was quite large. It stood strangely isolated from the surrounding huts, perhaps establishing a clear distinction between himself and his extended family or polygamous wives. The second distinction proved to be the case. Although the house was once bluish in color, it was now bordered by years of rain splashed mud stains. A reeking odor from constant urine against the wall bounced back with the stifling reek of ammonia.

Four very small hollow eyed tots, ashy skin, naked with tummies bulging from Kwashiorkor, were busying themselves with sticks for toys. They dabbled in an oozing stream of filth draining from a pipe at the side of the house. Obnoxious, disgusting blue bottle flies sipped from corners of their eyes, mouths, and noses.

There was another infant crawling toward an outhouse latrine which its door had swung open, thus emitting an unbearable odor. The latrine floor was covered with excreta. There was no flushing system, a mere hole in the ground.

The only child that took notice of me was the child that was crawling. He came toward me and held out what resembled a mud pie offering it to me. With disbelief I accepted it, hid it behind my back and quietly let it go. When I sniffed my fingers to check to see if whether or not it was mud, a little desperate prayer went up, "Please, Lord, Let it be!"

My worst fears were confirmed. It wasn't mud, I hurriedly grabbed my bag and opening my flask, douched my hands with water, and dried them. Another scary sniff. Just as I had thought, the filth was gone but the smell remained. What a lesson for life. What we do in this life may carry it's stench to our graves, and so perhaps the good may leave its fragrance. My lesson from a child. This lesson was rewarded by handing the little one a piece of peppermint. When he reached out his little elfish hand to take it, another surprise shook me. I jumped back when I noticed two large white body lice crawled from around his neck onto his chest. They actually seem to be following each other.

I teared up. "A down right disgusting shame!",! I thought. "Now *who is to blame?*"

The child laughed when I suddenly backed away. He thought that I was playing with him. I jumped back wards again to get another laugh out of him but suddenly, I found that my antics were not so amusing to the two mangy battle scared mongrels which showed up from the back of the house.

They came running toward me from around the back of the house. They were the toughest looking characters that I had ever seen on four legs. Parts of their noses and ears had been ripped off and it looked to me that they were targeting me for eyes, ears and nose replacements.

At that moment, I thought that I was a goner. These guys had earned their scars and stripes no doubt during their territorial meanderings when they clashed with wild boars and hyenas, specially those hyenas that love to prowl about the compounds at night. Dogs or no dogs, the hyenas are coming.

Whats next? I ask as my heart seem to stop. Inch by inch they crept closer, snarling, dagger teeth just waiting to sink into some fresh ghetto steak.

I folded the letter into a cylinder shape, hoping that it would appear as a deterrent. There I was, facing uncertain death by mongrels, ready to stab them to death with Tabby's letter of recommendation.

Suddenly, a loud, stern voice rang out. "Whiskey, Bombo get bak you stupid fellows, Is dis how you treat our guess?"

The animals slinked back, still growling.

This man of about thirty was Joseph, Chief Omubu's servant. Seeing that the dogs were still persistent, he shouted a word several times that set the dogs off in a hurry"forsaeka! forsaeka!" Off they went. The dogs understood that word and it worked every time. What it meant or how it affected them, I'll never know.

"Good afta noon, sah ," came the pleasant greeting.

"Good afternoon to you," I responded. Joseph was a very dark skinned, slender, short man walking bare footed. He was all smiles, his clothes a bit ragged and he displayed a warm hospitality.

"I'm here to see the Chief. Is he here?"

"No, sah, "Chief he don go fa college.""

"How far away is the college?"

"Oh, long way, long way. It be bout uh... kilometers don de road, sah," he said, not really saying exactly how far.

I had begun to wonder if I could survive another walk. Joseph spoke up. "You leave your bags here sah. I tak you through short path."

Joseph wasted no time in taking me down through a path that immediately brought us into an area of extremely tall elephant grass. The grass was sharp. blades lacerating. It was far worse than when I use to walk through that old corn field back in America many years ago, but the plague of bugs were nearly the same. Just at the moment when you would holler "ouch" from the slice of a blade, you could always count on a bug flying right in your mouth. Just don't make the mistake of suddenly taking that spontaneous bite unless you would shrug the thought of it off and consider it to be just another bit of protein.

It was about a half hour later that we stopped.

"Joseph, where are we now? How much farther?" I asked.

Joseph explained that we had entered onto the farm of another chief, Mukete by name. He assured me that we would arrive very shortly at the college. He kept saying, "small, small time sah."

I gazed up at the enormous razor sharp stalks arched

over head above us. It was an uneasy feeling for me. For the most part, the grass formed a canopy that literally blocked out the sun dark and gloomy.

"Uh, tell me Joseph, what is your surname?"

"Sah name sah?"

"Your last name?"

"Oh, last name be nah Bisong."

"Ok Joseph Bisong, good solid name." I exclaimed. "Tell me, Bisong, are there many snakes out here in this bush?"

"Snakes? Oh, we call them 'enjoka.' Oh, yes, yes, dey be p-l-e-n-t-y fa dis bush," Joseph exclaimed as he extended his arm, pointing in a swaying motion.

I glanced nervously about. Joseph seemed amused by my nervousness.

He continued, "Spitting enjoka, vipas, and de green mambas. If de bite you, eiiiyi! you go die one time fa dis ground,"

"All right, all right, you've made your point. Now let's get out of here," I insisted.

After some time we emerged from the bush onto M'Bong'e Road. It was then that we heard a roar of voices mingled with drum beats. As usual it was difficult to determine the direction from where the sound was coming.

Joseph assured me that it was perhaps someone at the college who had no doubt made a favorable announcement, which had merited the student's' voices and possibly the drum sounds.

As we came out of the tall bush onto MBonge Road, there was a tilted sign hanging on the fence that stretched the length of the front of the campus. On it was written in large, bold, fading black letters: RODGER'S FAIRCOURT COLLEGE, BAKE, KAMBA. Beneath it read:

"Chief V. Ngomo Omubu, Proprietor."

"Come." Joseph beckoned for me and pointed. "Dis be na Principal's office." He pointed to a tunnel aluminum sided building.

Some students crowed the entrance. Most of them were clamoring to keep their places in line as they waited to be heard. It could be seen right away from the elbowing and bickering among them that discipline was not a part of their syllabus. It was quite obvious that if it was ignored for long, a powder keg would explode. The thought came to me, I wonder who is really in charge here?

It was not that I was trying to be too critical at this stage, but coming from a military back ground, the very idea of discipline for any person, family, or group was always foremost in my mind. Of course, being disciplined is not always indicative of moral rectitude. Ask Hitler and his army, and they will answer you from Hades.

In spite of the loud clamor of shouts and even screams, the drums in the distance could still be heard. They seemed to be introducing a drama that was about to unfold.

The students were pressed together in line like sardines. The line extended about the length of a city block. They seemed quite content with the pushing and shoving. One student seemed to have gotten upset with another one and gave him a deliberate push. When he did, the entire line went backward and collapsed like dominoes. A few of them expressed anger, but the rest got a big laugh out of it. There was a girl who was heard berating a boy. While standing behind her, he decided to latch onto a sizable portion of her buttock and gave it a crushing squeeze. He then pretended to be innocently oblivious of his devilment as he gazed into the pure and undefiled heavens.

The girl was on to him. "You idiot!" she said as she spun around with an invective. "It t'was you who grabbed my butticones listen to me, I am not to be played with! I will have you beaten with a cobra! My father has power you know? He will have your stupid neck stretched like a giraffe." She then gave him a long, threatening stare and added, "Ha, you bush idiot! You bastard son of a bastard hippo!"

There was a strong possibility that the girl was not exaggerating about the boy being punished in that manner. It was later that I was to learn the truth.

I was assigned to witness a punitive action carried out by an enraged teacher at that same college. The student was flogged with a cane after he was caught stealing. He was suspected all along and was given ten strokes with a hippo cane. The boy was held down by his hands and knees on top of a table. He was thrashed so unmercifully that it made me quiver. Blood was drawn and he was treated with an ointment by the students that held him down. It was hard for me to get over it. My mind wasn't right for days. It actually affected my teaching performance. It was certainly not that type of discipline that I was opting for.

A few teachers who stood about the main building made no effort to bring about order. They were mere spectators standing listlessly about and commenting softly to each other now and then about certain students. I headed straight for the main building, assuming that the Chief might be there.

It was only later that I learned just how elusive he really was. In addition to his surprisingly small army of Bakunda tribesmen who served as vanguard to his private audience, I discovered that the Chief was heavily involved in witchcraft. I did not know it at the time, but I later figured it out. The Chief's witchcraft secrets would certainly be to his prompting. It would strike fear in some and convince the others surrounding him that he was actually supernaturally evasive. This would compound the superstitious phobias of his subjects toward him, but it would also unnerve them to carry out his bidding.

Politely elbowing my way through the crowd, I opened the door. Inside was a small hallway with adjacent offices on both sides. On a grey door was a stenciled sign: Head Mistress, Mrs. Diop. Beneath it read: "Knock twice, wait to be told to enter."

I knocked twice, softly, then waited. There was no answer. I gave two more gentle knocks. This time a bit louder. Still there was no answer. My American impatience was kicking in. I slowly opened the creaky door and walked into a small, congested office. The desk in front of me was piled with moldy papers. Behind it sat a short, thin, nearly chinless Caucasian woman. She seemed tired.

Not looking up at first, she stormed, "Did you not read the sign? It says wait to be told to enter!"

"My apologies, Madame." I answered.

She looked up. The moment that she saw me, her face reddened. She appeared surprised. Perhaps justifiably so. it certainly was not my intention. I too was somewhat surprised since the name Diop was African. It was like two people of different ethnic origins meeting each other for the very first time in the most unexpected place. I would describe it as being something like being caught for the space of three heart beats between suspended emotions. I smiled.

"And what can I do for you?" she asked with a slightly stern expression.

I may have been a bit paranoid at the time, but for some reason, I had an over whelming feeling that she had been informed in advance that I was coming there, but she had not been told that I was a black American.

I extended my hand. She shook it slightly.

"I'm Tyler Holiday. I'm wondering if you could direct me to Chief Omubu?"

Looking over her glasses, she asked "And why do wish to see the Chief? I'm here to run his affairs."

I started to answer. "Well, I, uh…." She broke in. "Looking for employment, I suppose?"

"Well, yes, I…."

"Teaching, I suppose?"

"Y yes, teaching."

"Where are you from?" She asked.

"America," I responded.

Then the word rang out in my mind: rival! Could that be what she felt?

"What brings you here to Africa?" came the question. "Tracing your roots, I suppose." She sniggled.

"Not really," I answered. "From what I have seen here in Africa, so far, there are far more crucial matters for a man to be concerned about than digging up his sixteenth century roots."

I felt some resentment in her interrogation or at least that's what I took it to be. Through the years I had learned to curb my tongue. Prudence with a little patience might reveal another man's motive. Maybe that was Diop's way of testing me. I then asked her where she was from.

She said that she was from Scotland. She then quickly changed the subject. "What subject do you teach?"

I would say counseling for starters with a document as a follow up. "Religion, History," I answered, then added, "I've also worked as a counselor."

She was mistaken when she said, "No need for counselors here. We have to see something tangible from anybody who comes here to teach. Besides, I doubt if there is anything like counseling that is officially endorsed in the whole of Africa."

She continued, "The Ministry of Education requires that all expatriates from Great Britain and America teach English as a second language. English is required to be taught in addition to whatever subjects you may have majored in. It saves the government from paying for extra English Instructors. They try to get as much out of expats as they can. So you think that you can handle English?"

Before I could respond, she cut in, "But you Americans

don't speak proper English, especially you blacks."

"Well, Mrs. Diop, that may be partly true because there is a great deal of illiteracy in America, but from listening to the British and the Scottish speak over the years, I have discovered that the King's English over there is a lost art. Our rhetoric in America does not lie in our proper use of the English language, so much as it is in our ability to stand up for Great Britain and Scotland against the tyranny of Germany, which, by the way, we are still willing to do to protect the Sovereignty of those nations."

Mrs. Diop seemed to think it over. "I suppose you're right" "But you had better talk employment over with the Chief. He has the final say. He is the only one that can hire you."

"So, where can I find the Ch...?"

She broke in. "When you go out of this building, turn left and keep straight down the path past the girl's dormitory. You'll most likely find the chief down by the piggery. Follow the smell. You can't miss it. I'd take you there myself but I hate those filthy creatures. They make me sick to my stomach. He has a new breed of pigs that he is experimenting with. I never go that way, can't stand the stench. The Chief and I have many a fallen-out over those swine. They are going to be the ruin of this college. By, the way, should the Chief hire you, I give you fair warning. Never, ever say anything against those swine to him. He will fly into a rage and have you kicked out of this college. For some reason he has the strangest obsession with those animals beyond the cravings of any human that I have ever known. I can't exactly put my finger on it, but it's the closest thing to a fetish or a religion as I have ever seen.

Mrs. Diop looked at me for a moment. She seemed as though she wanted to get a lot off of her chest.

"If you happen to get employment here with us," she said, "I will be in a better position to discuss it with you in more detail. For now, I will simply say that I hope that you soon realize what you are getting yourself into by trying to work here. This is a private college. It is not ran by the government, although we are required to meet government regulations and arrange our syllabuses accordingly."

It was as though the Head Mistress had been waiting to find someone that she could talk to. When two foreigners occasionally meet, whether it is in Africa or in some other economically emerging country, there seems to be a westernized type of compatibility, especially if they both speak English.

She continued. "We are trying our damnedest to get the Chief to pay his teachers their salaries. He goes for months at a time without paying us. This is really hurting our staff and it also effects the morale of the students."

She pointed out of the window at a few students. Then commented "They have worked so hard to maintain their Self Reliant Projects and perform in their classes at the same time."

There was a sad, motherly look in her watery eyes. She cleared her throat.

"By the way," she said. Your counseling would be no competition with the witch doctors and their methods. Never the less, like I said, you talk it over with the Chief."

CHAPTER 10

SHORT LIFE OF CONTROL

As I reached for the door to leave the office, Mrs. Diop stopped me.

"Again," she asked, "What is your name? full name?"

It's "Holiday, maam, Tyler Holiday, and may I ask your full name?"

While scribbling my name on a tablet, she answered, "Mrs. Flora Bisong Diop. I prefer to be called Mrs. Diop, although the students and the staff address me as "Madame."

A second effort to leave the office was interrupted by two knocks on the door.

Mrs. Diop ignored it, as she had my knock. They knocked again.

"Well, come in, come in," she yelled impatiently.

The door opened slightly and one eye peeked around.

"Well don't just stand there peeking like a plastered… What is it that you want?"

A very short man slowly entered the room. He was slightly bent over as a customary gesture of respect. It was something quite common in Africa.

I was soon to learn that Diop, although she appeared to be quite abrasive in her demeanor, was never the less a favorite of the students. They were very loyal to her. They were also aware of her frustrations with the Chief and his constant interference with her administration. The students needed her leadership and she provided it for them. At first it was difficult for me to understand her manner. I was actually put off by it, but I was later put at ease as I realized that the students took no offense at it. To most of them she was a mother away from home. This, of course was one of the examples of how patience, walking hand in hand with prudence, may provide the revelation of a motive. Not all motives are secretly hidden. Some of them are camouflaged within plain view.

The office door opened wider. In stepped two others.

"Good afternoon Madame," speaking simultaneously.

Diop called to me, "Holiday, wait, Boys, meet Mr. Holiday. he's from America. Perhaps he will be working for us soon."

"Ohooo," came the replies.

Diop spoke. "That is, if the Chief can find a place for him. Mr. Holiday, meet Mr. Ekoko, our Vice Headmaster, Mr. Tandangu, our Bursar, and Mr. Eta, our Recreations Officer." The men extended their hands.

"Welcome to our country!" Eta said.

Mr. Ekoko joined in, "And how do you find our little country certainly not to be compared to a developed country such as your America."

"Mmm, on the contrary, Mr. Ekoko," I said. "I think that your country is by far among the most beautiful I have seen. If beauty is in the eye of the beholder, then I have truly beheld the beauty. And besides, if I were you, I wouldn't bother so much about the size of this precious jewel of yours, geographical ramifications are always significant. No one would challenge history's claims on that topic. I believe what's more important are the dimensions of peace. That is something that America has to fight for every day. Peace without and peace within. These days, even America has to sleep with one eye open."

We laughed.

"Sounds as though we have an orator in our midst." Tandangu remarked.

"No, no," I answered. "I'm far from being an orator, just telling it like it is."

Mrs. Diop remained reticent the entire time, observant, but reticent. The beating of the drums became more audible.

I asked "By the way, gentlemen, tell me about the drums. Do they ever stop beating? Not that I have anything against them, of course, but it is the mystery about them that stirs my curiosity. They can be heard all the time, everywhere, even through the night and during the early morning. Yet it seems so impossible to locate them."

Tandangu spoke in a way that I will never forget. "Mr. Holiday, drums are the heartbeat of black Africa. Should the drums cease to beat, Africa will die."

The cheerful men turned toward their Headmistress.

One of them asked, "Has Madame taken her flask of tea this afternoon?"

She answered with a slight frown, "Certainly not. As a matter of fact, that Mukete hasn't served it to me this entire day."

Looks of disappointment crossed their faces.

"I'll get that rascal on the ball right away, Madame!" Mr. Eta said as he spun toward the door yelling, "Mukete, Mukete!" With further disgust he complained, "Why isn't he ever around when he is needed?"

He pointed to the nearest student that crammed the door. "You, boy, go and fetch Mukete tell him to come immediately with Madame's tea and be quick about it!" He then muttered, "What is the matter with this man? He has one small assignment and can't do it!"

Like a dry sponge, Diop seem to have gotten a kick out of receiving so much attention. It showed when her face lit up with a smile. The two men that remained in her office sensed their triumph in it, further commented, "When I was coming along just a few years ago, I would have seen to it that very man was thrashed for not having Madame's tea on time." He then faced me with the remark: "Mr. Holiday, you see what independence has done to our people? It has made them lazy."

"Well," I answered, "I can clearly see why under neo-colonialism there is still no rest for the weary, but unnecessary nostalgia for institutional thrashing."

I left it at that., hoping that he would catch on.

With a glance at the Headmistress, I thought, This ole

girl, a real queen bee right here in the abdomen of Africa. What an accomplishment!

"Boys," Diop said, "Take Mr. Holiday to the Chief and you get right back here to me. I have matters to discuss with you."

We started to leave.

"Wait!," she said. "On second thought, Tandangu, you escort him. The two of you remain here with me."

Passing through the throng of students with Tandangu in the lead, we came face to face with Mukete, the servant. His body appeared to be slightly bent over but he was nevertheless at his best, prodding his way through the throng as he attempted to balance the silver tray of hot water above the student's heads.

Tandangu spoke brashly. "Mukete, you fool!"

Mukete nervously stood his ground. "I am not tay fool, sah, It t'was Amelia, de girl fa de house. She be no mak-um hot wata fa tea sah. I be late. It's not my fault, sah."

There was a spark of pride in Mukete's retort. With my expanded imagination I would like to think that at least there still lay dormant beneath that black, perspiring bosom the burning embers that once flamed the war cries of his ancestors. You may call them Mau Mau fires, Mandela fires, Kenyetta fires or even Shaka fires. Call them anything you like, but give Mukete a noble name. Allow him to bask with pride beneath the African sun. Let him live and die with the dignity that God ordained for him to have and bestowed upon him from his infant breath.

Let him dance with pride to the drum beats of undaunted

warriors, Let him live with a noble name and die with a noble spirit. For a man with a noble spirit can never die as a fool. Although poverty had fallen to his lot and he has accepted the lowest position of servitude, he should never be called a fool for doing it. I saw a man who, if called on would not hesitate to serve his country.

I couldn't help asking that age old question, "Where is the justice in this world?"

Human justice is blind in one eye and racism is blind in both. It is a difficult truth to swallow but the fact remains that on both sides of the Atlantic there are men who actually despise their own human dignity by despising the human dignity of others. From the moment that it sprang into their consciousness, they prefer the darkness of their mother's womb and confirm it by living their earthly lives, warring aggressively against the light of love. From cradle to grave, they are enamored with the blackest depravity. They hate their mothers for forcing them into the light and they, in turn, despise with a passion the children of light. Such men should be sought after and destroyed. From what I have observed through all these years, the dignity of the human race is obligated to do so.

Tandangu said, "The Chief has been Proprietor of this college for quite a few years now and all that he has ever cared about is the money that it brings to him from the student's fees and from its self-reliant program."

The longer he talked, the more irate he became. He began showing it by shaking his cane.

"That Program was spread across Africa by the Peace

Corps but when they pulled out of this place, the Chief took it over and added more pigs. He then took the food that the students were growing for themselves and gave it to his relatives to sell for him at the market. They bring all of the money to him. The student's parents are struggling to pay their fees for room and board. But when the Bursar counts the money, always in the Chief's presence, he just snatches it up and off he goes. When this happens, the Teachers are paid less than half their salaries. He orders the Bursar to give them promissory notes but they never see the money,"

There was much disgust and understandable resentment coming from the Assistant Headmaster. If what he was saying was the truth, it was worthy of war. He had much more to say.

"The teachers are always threatening to quit. Besides all of this, the maintenance of this school is falling apart. Roofs leak in rainy season, rats eat student's rice, weevils invade their beans, mosquitoes suck the life out of unprotected dormitories and in dry season there is a terrible water shortage. No water, just the overflowing outhouses."

He then added: "How awful they smell. The Chief has no academic interest, but he is a very clever man, one that you never want to cross. I have actually seen men missing who have attempted it."

The Headmaster stopped to cool off. "Sorry, Mr. Holiday, forgive me for venting. But let's not discuss the Chief any farther. In time, should you work for us, you will get to know more than you need to know about him.

As we walked, my frustrated tour guide latched his little finger on to mine. In Africa it is a gesture of friendship and is customary in vast areas of the continent. I never got accustomed to it, but I was wary not to be offensive.

With the majority of the students far behind us, Tandangu and I could now hear each other more clearly. "You must not mind them staring at you, Mr. Holiday. They are not accustomed to seeing any one like you. We can't grow hair like that here. The climate is too hot."

I explained to Tandangu that during my travels from Cairo to Tanzanian and west, over into Victoria, most of which was by land, I saw many tribes, people with long hair,

"Fulani, a few Ethiopians, Wadobi and even Masai. It's not a matter of taste," I added. "It's a matter of climatic adaptation, maybe genetic migration, I suppose, give or take a strand or two."

Tandangu laughed. Then looking at me seriously he asked, "But you're not an African, Mr. Holiday...are you?"

How clear were the ancient words of Joseph, came echoing back from what I had read in the Book of Genesis, when after twenty years, his own brothers mistook him for an Egyptian. "'I am Joseph, your brother, whom ye sold into Egypt." Well I am Holiday, your brother, whom ye sold into America.

"Now, now, Tandangu," I cautioned." I am not an African by nationality, but I am by race. I should think that you as a teacher should know the answer to that one. Your history of Africa is not complete without me. Until our arms are long enough to join hands for a bridge across the Atlantic, we will always be estranged brothers. We should take the word "divide" out of "Divide and Conquer!" We need to conquer our ignorance about our true relationship, our true history, and conquer our political barriers. "The only racial differences that any race has are the ones that racist have created for themselves and us."

About half way across the campus, a group of students had gathered in our path just ahead of us. They showed fear of Tandangu. The group broke up and a few of them could be seen running. I was told later that the senior Prefects often used the junior students as lookouts who kept tabs on every move that he made. This particular day, the students were aware that Tandangu was preoccupied with showing me around the campus, which no doubt provided them with the leverage they needed to indulge in whatever promiscuities that were available to the nearly five hundred of them, he explained.

There were a lot of sex acts. A few girls had gotten pregnant, he told me. There were also quite a few thefts, hardly any brawls, but a great deal of expulsions for cheating in final exams. Those were adamant grounds for a no return policy.

The Headmaster gave me a sly glance. He was aware that I had noticed the student's strange, uncomfortable behavior in his presence. Instinctively he came up with an explanation for it.

"This is the only way that you can control them, Mr. Holiday." Without warning, he gave a few swift, air cutting swooshes with his long, tan, flexible hippo hide cane. It had been tucked under his arm since we had left the office.

It sounded familiar. "Daddy Brew," I had learned while traveling the land, used to wield this type of cane when he issued penalties by court order, and also by some of his white missionaries who pioneered with him through Africa. He used this punitive instrument in his sick effort to brand the Kingdom of God into the backs of Africans instead of loving it into their hearts.

"You see, Mr. Holiday, we Africans..." Tandangu hesitated. "Well, let me put it in this way I think that the hot sun in this part of the world has cooked our brains. The only language that the African student seems to understand is the language of the cane!"

I had heard that kind of talk before. I had read it in books written by whites such as Rhodes, the German Princes who forced the Africans to build their castles, and Jan Smuts before the Battle of Blood River cost him the very same fate that Custer faced at Little Bighorn.

But to hear it come from the mouth of an African simply evidence the indelible imprint left behind by eighteenth century arrogance. It was "spare the rod, spoil the child."

In their eyes, the African never became a man. He was always, and forever, the primitive child who could never mature beyond the scepter of the cane. Africa still wears the scars of a sadomasochistic suzerainty.

"It's true, it's true," the Headmaster emphasized as he became more insistent. "I know the African. These are my people. I am a part of them. You talk to an African nicely and what will you get? Ha! He will not respect your authority. He will see you only as a fool."

After noticing my look of strong disapproval, he reinforced his point.

"They will not give you your due respect. They can even steal from you. The answer is fear, fear, fear. That is the tactic that you must use."

I had heard about enough of Tandangu's methods, and realizing that a few of the students were listing in brought on me a strong feeling of embarrassment.

"Well, Mr. Tandangu, you have expressed your feelings and I am quite sure that you are resolved to your philosophy of fear and punishment although what you say might work in most cases but not for long. I, on the other hand, must hold to the premise that the African has been up against insurmountable challenges since the collapse of colonial days and those challenges brought unavoidable hardships. Someday he will grow tired of 'care box' sympathy, foreign paternalism and exported domination. Nobody stays oppressed forever."

I thought it time to change the subject slightly. "You know, Mr. Tandangu. Just between you and me, I haven't met the Chief as yet What do you think he would have to say about all of this school discipline? After all, this is his school."

Tandangu showed resentment in his face. "The Chief?" He caught himself putting his hand over his mouth, realizing that he had spoken too loudly.

"Don't make me laugh, sah."

He leaned toward me with his hand still to his mouth and whispered, "That man could care a dam about the reputation of this school. I am one of his tribe's men. I know him. He sees the students only as slaves. They tend his every need, his crops, his chickens, his coffee plantation, his palm wine. All of this he has taken away from them. Those were supposed to be the student's projects...and the pigs. Oh my goodness! I can't even believe myself what I am about to tell you. The Chief is in love with those dam swine. They are everything to him, his world. He plays with them, he sings to them, and he even serves them wine, good wine! A woman that he went to bed with once told me that he even has a photograph of his first pig hanging over his bed. Can you believe that? How do you think she felt to be sexing the Chief and suddenly she looked up and there was this very big pig staring her in the face? And then she looked down at the Chief and couldn't tell the difference."

Tandangu talked on, nonstop. "The Chief is bribing the school Inspectors not to come around. They meet with him at his house, he tells them all they need to know about the school, serves them up with food, wine and dancers and they all go away as happy as a porcupine with his quills stuck up their buttocks."

CHAPTER 11

THE KWASHIORKER CHIEF

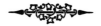

Tandangu suddenly tapped me on the shoulder.
"There he is," He whispered with excitement. "There
be the Chief," he continued as his hand trembled pointing
to the direction of the pigpen.

I could tell that Tandangu was terrified. His hands trembled. His words became unclear. He unhooked his finger
quickly from mine. He was showing the same fear toward
the Chief that he had preached so boldly about.

He then added slyly, "I believe it more appropriate that
you introduce yourself. I will discuss matters with you later."

With those words, Tandangu hurried off in the direction of the Head Mistres's office.

"Hey! Wait a minute, I...."

I looked around and he was gone. I could have used
him for at least a couple of seconds longer to tell me how to
approach a Chief.

From a distance, I stretched my neck to get a better
look. It wasn't working. The brilliant sun was too blinding.

I walked closer. The unbearable odor from the pigs became worse. It didn't take too much imagination to taste the stench. In Africa, the heat brings the essence of everything and everybody to the surface. Even from that distance, I would no doubt carry the lingering smell back home with me in my clothes.

I squinted my eyes against the sun, to take another cautious look and there, leaning over a low sagging fence that surrounded the piggery, silhouetted in the dark shade of the branches of banana leaves, rested a short, tubby, potbellied Bakundu man, the Chief himself.

His glossy indigo blue-black skin gave tribute to the true title: "Son of the Sun." From the reputation that preceded him, it was my worst fears that his attitude toward me in the coming days would not brand him with the label "The Merciless Son of the Merciless Sun."

While gazing at this man who was so short in statue, so kwashiorkor in appearance, one could hardly believe that this was the Chief who had stood so defiantly on the steps of his country's Capital and defied the Parliament, cursed the status quo to the high heavens, and allegedly swindled their national treasury. Now here he stood, bowing in submission to the very swine that he fell in love with, that is, to the dire neglect of all others including his own little lice infested children that groveled so pitifully on the ground of his own compound.

A layer of blubber rested at the back of his nearly neckless shoulders. He wore a toboggan cap that hugged his fat little head. About his protruding belly draped a brilliant yellow wrapper that was designed with red polka dots which flowed down to his ankles and nearly touched the ground.

An electrifying tenor voice spoke out with a strong accent. "Ah ha, Mista Holiday!" His short arms aimed toward the pigs. "Just look at dem, de pigs, Are dey not beautiful? Look at dem. I love dem."

The Chief turn to me while still pointing at his pigs. Already, he knew my name.

"Do you know why I love dem, Mista Holiday? Unlike humans dey have nothing to hide. Dey are true to deyer nature. If dey want to grunt...dey grunt. If dey want to squeal... dey squeal. If dey want to sheet, dey don't have to fly all de way ober to Nigeria to buy toilet paper. dey just stand where dey are and let de ground have it. After dey do it, dey just lay down in it and cool off. Dey don't even wash dem selves, because if dey did, dey would go and flop back down in it again. So what's dey use? Dey don't have a constitution. Dey don't follow rules. Dey don't get sick. Not even snakes can kill dem. Most of all," The Chief paused, looked at me sternly. His dark eyes were penetrating, making sure that he had my attention.

"Most of all, dey neva, neva challenge me, like some of de donkeys on my staff."

I got the hint. The message was clear. Now I would learn how he really felt about those pigs.

"Do you see dat beautiful mama ober dere?" he asked as he pointed over to a four hundred pound sow lying on her side. Her enormous body rocked from side to side from the pushing of her voracious litter of seven as they yanked furiously at her teats.

"She is Fumi. I sing to her. De oder one beside her is her oldest daughter, Pundu. She is already pregnant....And deya is Fumyta, Tesima, Pesimdo and Mebi."

There was great delight in the Chief's face as he proudly introduced me to his pigs. But then his face really lit up.

"But de bery, bery huge one laying ober dere in corner with de bery large testicles." He pointed to a boar that far outweighed the sow. "I call him Papa Childs.... Do you know why I call him Papa Childs, Mista Holiday? It tis because he is de Great papa of all dees childs yes, dey are all his childs."

Upon recognizing his name, Papa Childs raised his gigantic head, gave the Chief a muddy salute with his snout and with a short grunt, flopped his fat head back into the mud.

From the time of my arrival, I had learned from the Headmistress that there was a war between her and the Chief, a war that had raged long before my coming.

During my initial talk with the Chief, he made it quite clear that there was no love lost between the two of them. None of this undercurrent was in the best interest of all parties concern, especially the students. The Chief had informed me on that very first day that as far as he was concern, Mrs. Diop was there at his school only for ornamental purposes.

I saw it differently. She had become a galvanizing entity who had won the students over. The fact that she had married one of their fellow Africans had completely sealed their trust in her. To them she was there to stay, with hardly any chance of her ever leaving them and going back to Europe. The commitment that she had made was not only to her husband but it was a pledge to them as well.

The Chief was adamant about his feelings. As a Chief, he had been challenged and was losing.

"She came to dis kontry as a volunteer with dey teacha's Training College in Baktumba," He said. "At de time, her name was Braninigan . A few days afta wads she was seen dancing and partying all ober de place. Our men came from miles around and were chasing her about like porcupines afta a warthog."

It was something that the Chief had to get off of his chest. He had to finish the story.

"It was our women who figured it out." he said. "It was dey who realized dat it was deyar men who had neva gotten dat close to a white woman before. Dey became so afraid dat she would steal dayer husbands dat dey reported de matta to de local gendarmerie, but since dey were also enjoying her, dey ignored de complaints."

Chief Omubu summarized his story by adding that the now Headmistress had at one time caused such a scandal that the authorities were pressured to ask her to leave the country either that or she would have been deported by force. That was when she met up with a Mister Bisong Diop, a tribesman of the Chief and a common farmer living near his school.

Before he married her, he went to the Chief and ask for his blessing. The Chief tried to no avail to talk him out of it. The woman had stolen his heart. He told the Chief that he was mesmerized by her white skin, and that for him it would be a chance of a lifetime. It was later, as the Chief had explained, that in spite of her not having a degree, he went on to hire her.

It was an awful lot of revelation for me to have received in one day, but in Africa, every body's life is an open book to everyone else. It is almost a matter of public record. If you write in it, they will read it. If it happened, it is as if they read it in the newspapers.

My curiosity had been put to rest. Now I knew to an extent just why it was that so many of the employees were bold and eager to give me a heads up about the Chief. My being a total stranger in their midst was of little importance. To them, the more you know about a person, the less of a stranger you become.

It is something like joining your fellow soldiers on the enemy line. Once you have been briefed about the strategy of the battle, you are qualified to engage in it. In the case of the teachers, it was a battle for consensus.

It's universal. Get hired on any job, eat in any company cafeteria, attend any church, night club or prison and consensus will tug at you for the mastery.

It was now apparent that there was a vicious rivalry between the Chief and the Headmistress. What was even more apparent was that it was becoming more transparent as the dark cloud of contention loomed across the African forecast.

Chief Omubu directed me to escort him over to a large log. He couldn't stand for very long, but he wanted to talk.

"I suppose you are wondering how it tis dat I know your

name" he said cunningly. I was about to speak.

"No one can take me, de Chief by surprise, Mista Holiday. I have eyes and ears everywhere. From de time dat you left your taxi at de market, I knew dat you were here in my kontry."

He dropped silent, giving me a quick once-over with shifty eyes. I said nothing.

I know that it sounds pretty hypocritical but there are times when a man has to pretend to be humble even if he is not by nature.

The Chief slapped both of his thighs.

"But first, let us discuss business." he said.

"I unda stand dat you have come a long way to see me. What brings you heya, since you have come all de way from America across de great pond by plane? What do you want of me?"

"Well, Chief," I answered, "I have traveled over much of Africa and now I have come this distance in search of employment, perhaps to teach. My intentions are to settle in Africa. You know, to become acquainted with your ways and your customs. I have a letter of recommendation from one of your former colleagues, Mr. Tabby in Victoria. I…"

The Chief held up his hand for silence. He was show-ing me who was in charge. That was lesson number one. Maintain silence whenever a Chief shoves his hand in your face.

"Oh yes, Tabby my good friend of de Pa-la-ment days. How is he dees days?"

I handed the letter to him.

With a deep grunt, the Chief stared at it, actually for quite some time. I discovered later that he was not illiterate. It was just that it couldn't be proven by his pronounced accent. Finally, he cleared his throat, only this time with an air of importance.

"I tink I could use a man like you. Did you bring your particulars?"

"I did, Chief, My Bachelor's Degree in…" Again, he held up his hand.

"I have been advised by de Provincial Delegate for Education dat I should have at least one person who is a degree- holder on my staff, but up till now, I have not been able to find a single person. I tink it's because we are too far out in de bush. We cannot pay enough and besides, nobody ever comes dis way."

It sounded to me that the Chief's interview with me was in the reverse.

I spoke up. "But what of your Headmistress, Mrs. Diop doesn't she…?"

His hand went up, this time in frustration. "Oh, her." came the dry interruption. This time the Chief's voice was filled with disgust. His face showed resentment.

"Diop?" he said. "She has no degree. I merely employed her because she is white. I felt dat it would add prestige to my college. In dis part of Africa, white people are rare and white women are even more scarce." He hesitated. "We need de whites, Mista Holiday. Even now dey business men and women from Europe and America are helping to run the governments of Africa. Perhaps someday de whole of Africa will unite and walk on her own two feet."

"Do you mean to say, Chief, that they are working with Africans as Advisors?

He held up his hand. "No," he said. "Not as advisors, Dey are making our policies. From government, international to dey law of de seas. We Africans have no banks of our own. Only in name. We do not print our monies. Our medicines are shipped in from Germany. Sometimes dey bring our medicines to de Gulf of Equatorial Guinea and just drop it off with nobody to collect it and go back to dere ships. De supplies set on de beach fa days because people are afraid to pick it up. I believe dat it is experimental medicine. If it don't kill us, it won't kill de Germans."

The Chief spoke like a seasoned politician. You could tell that the Parliament blood was still in his veins. The shrewdness, the cunning were still there. But he had not learned it from the Parliament. It was inherent. He would always be attempting to check mate.

I wanted to get his version of how he went from the Parliament to the pigs. I wanted to know it from him but I knew that I dare not to cross that threshold.

"On de whole," the Chief continued, "We Africans have to be friendly to everybody. We are in de center of a nuclear camp. We are de only people in de world who has not gone nuclear." He then chuckled and added: "So having a white woman, to us, is like having a nuclear bomb. We sometimes send her places to beg for money for us, but she seldom brings very little of it back."

There were two farm hands strolling across the compound. "Hey you, dere!" the Chief shouted. "Come heya, you idiots!"

The men ran to the Chief as fast as they could and kneeled. The Chief pointed to some rickety carts. "Take dees two carts and run to my house. Have Joseph fill dem with mimbo and bring dem back to my pigs. Go quickly."

I recalled that mimbo was palm wine. I knew better than to question the Chief about it, but it was nonetheless unbelievable. After watching the Chief on watering his swine with mimbo, I quickly put it to poetry in my head: "Somewhere deep in Africa, there's a Chief who loves his swine.

He sings to them and plays with them and even serves them wine."

I felt at the time that the poem was somewhat curt but fitting.

"We are happy to have our black brothers return to Africa. Deyar hardly any in our country. All those who come are welcome. We will even give dem as much land as dey need, as long as dey come in peace." The Chief shook his finger, threatening. "But we do not tolerate dem coming here as spies!"

The conversation ended with the Chief assuring me that my position at the college would not in any way conflict with the Headmistress' performance. I would be teaching and assisting with the proper planning of the school's compound. Sharing a few of my ideas that I might have picked up in the states would be another one of my functions and of course, whenever possible, I would assist with writing a few proposals for grants for the College.

"You can fill out an application for employment in de morning," he said. "In de meantime, I will have Atasi here to show you to your living quarters. Atasi, it's the one next to de Vice Principal's house."

"Yissah," a young man who was with us answered.

CHAPTER 12

A HOUSE AT LAST

Without speaking another word, the Chief made a few grunts as he struggled to raise himself up with his stick. He then waddled back toward his piggery as he yelled, "Pundu, you naughty girl, what did you do to make yourself pregnant, eh? I will bring you mimbo so dat you will bring happy babies into dis world."

The Chief was a strange man. His brown eyes were penetrating and soul reading, perhaps in search of anything salvageable worth manipulating. Cleverness was among his paramount master crafts. He was definitely not someone to be taken for granted or even dare to cross. To attempt to finagle one's way into his favor would no doubt require such merits of exhaustion that even the darkest of demons would hesitate to pounder.

I must admit that during our entire conversation, it was a bit unsettling. But for now, I would have to concentrate on being settled in, and getting acquainted with the staff, the students and my new environment.

Atasi and I arrived at my new living quarters. There was not anything on the outside of the house that suggested a welcome. That task would be left for me to create.

The house, just as with all the other buildings, was a dull, unpainted structure of mud covered with cement. Large spaces of missing white wash and chipped cement exposed the mud. The house had no windows of glass, only some rust- brown, sun scorched shutters. The torturous mosquitoes had free access to the inside.

Standing very close to the side of the house was a tall tree that I was told to be considered one of the most dangerous in Africa, although I never learned its name. It was very stout and its basketball size fruit was inedible. Occasionally, its fruit would come hurling to the ground with a cannon ball thud. They have killed a few people. When I asked why the tree had not been cut down, I was informed that it was a sacred tree and to destroy it would bring bad luck. I simply responded by mentioning that I couldn't think of any worse luck than to have the day lights knocked out of you by one of its fruits.

Atasi opened the creaky door of my new place. A gust of mold hit my nose. It had been approximately nine months since it was last occupied. We walked in, swiping thick webs. There were three rooms to explore. I looked up at the tin roof. There was no ceiling, only dar- brown rafters that supported the roof extended overhead from wall to wall. I got an eerie feeling when I saw several species of the largest spider, just short of tarantula size, clinging tenaciously to their geometric webs that were attached to the rafters. They shook with a frenzy at the slightest disturbances. Those webs were strong enough to trap a small bird. There were also a few bats hanging from the rafters.

The grey, peeled painted walls caught my attention when they came to life with geckos. They were everywhere darting about. When I moved they would move to get out of my away.

Many a night or morning since that day, I would jerk from feeling something cold and rubbery sliding against my thigh or leg. When I would throw back my sheet, there it would be a gecko that had fallen from the wall. I was just praying that my bed partner wasn't a cobra, which was common in the area.

I ask the typical city boy question, not being familiar with geckos. "Are these things poisonous?"

Atasi laughed. "No Sah, not poison."

"Doubtful," I muttered. "Might as well get used to it. Back in the states, I was just dying to get to Africa. Now here I am with a double dose of it."

I passed through a narrow corridor into what would be my bedroom. A filthy mattress laid on the box spring. There were dried urine stains on it and did it reek! Right there on the wall were dried dark red splotches. Other similar spots were smeared. I called Atasi.

"Sah?"

"Tell me, what is this on the wall?"

He poked his head around the corner of the room. "Oh, dat be na blood, sah."

"Blood? I paniced. What blood? Whose blood?"

"Yisah," Atasi added. "blood." He smiled, scratching his head. "blood from mosquito bites. Dey be plenty bad here, sah. Dey teachers who use to stay here, dey smack-um fa wall wid dey hands, sah."

I figured it out. Teacher after teacher who used this room over the years simply smashed those blood suckers against the wall with their hands and left the blood there for the next teachers to smash his share of the same. This practice continued until finally the wall resembled a Picasso. Of course, this was not done for artistic reasons, but it was what it added up to.

A walk into the rest room stirred a swarm of flies. It was all I could do to keep them out of my face. Naturally, they were attracted to the odor. No one had flushed it, apparently due to water shortage. There were feces on both the floor and the wall. I took it that by passers had taken advantage of the place because it had been vacant for so long. But that was not the case.

"Atasi," I yelled. "This has to be cleaned. You mean to tell me that…."

Atasi interrupted. "Dey just taken-um fa finga en fling-urn fa wall, sah."

"Ok! ok!" I said. "I've got your point. Will you please go and clean this and the blood off for me?"

"Yissah," Atasi answered. "I go clean um tomorrow."

"No sir," I insisted. "You go clean-um today. Now."

Atasi trotted off on winged ankles in search of cleaning supplies.

It was impossible to express how tired I was tired from

the long journey from Victoria, tired from the long walk to the school, and drained by the burning sun.

Nothing short of rest could do me any good.

At the end of the day, I flopped down on the uncovered mattress. I would press Atasi the next day to get me a fresh one. About 2:30 a.m., the scream of a bush baby woke me. The little night marsupial's cry was so shrill that as it became louder, my eardrums vibrated. It finally stopped only after it had appeared to have been sitting on my shoulder.

I lit a candle that was nearly burnt out. Before long its dying flicker cast an eerie glow on the wall across the room. A mild breeze entered the through the shutters. I walked over to close them. It was then that I heard the luring sound of those distant drums again.

I promised myself that someday, I would find their mysterious source. The candle burned out. I stood in the dark, still listening to the drums. I lit another candle and laid back down across the bed. The beady-eyed rats stared at me from the rafters above, showing no fear. Nobody had ever chased them before.

In Africa, it's live and let live. I felt that the slogan had gone too far, especially as it applied to the mosquitoes that would not let me rest. Those were the creatures that conquered the slave traders, and the missionaries who came to Africa.

They had Stanley Livingston, Alfred Saker and Daddy Brew, lying on their backs with scorching fever gasping for breath. Many men have been taken from Africa as slaves by conquerors armed with muskets, whips, ropes, yokes and chains. If all of this could be put into a symphony, it would reverberate the loudest thunder and cast the blackest cloud across the skies. But no man is a match against the humming orchestras that are played in the minor key by the anopheles and various mosquitoes. Even to this day they are sending armies of Africans to their untimely graves.

The rats were "Goliath Rats," using the rafters as cross walks. Whether they were harmless or not, I still found it difficult to go back to sleep. In America, if a rat should get into your house, you wouldn't rest until it was dead. Here in Africa, in your home, they are merely ecology's tenants. In Africa they are saying "We have just as much right to be in your home as does that scorpion that is about to crawl off the wall onto your shoulder."

Never the less I ask myself "Why?" Why the rats? Why the lizards? And why are the mosquitoes in my house?" I finally figured it out. The people supplied blood for the mosquitoes, the lizards fed on them, the rats and lizards played king of the rafters, while they all were cautious to avoid the deadly spider webs below.

It was all about facing the realities of Africa. Those realities were soon to increase in magnitude. I was a tiny actor on the great stage of Africa's theater far from being at the center of that stage, but just somewhere far to the side, nearly invisible, a tiny speck that had blown back across the vast ocean to find its identity in its indigenous soil.

The feeling of being accepted on the college staff was a joy short lived. I had a job to perform. A feeling of uneasiness gripped me when the sudden thought that I might in some way disappoint my students. Would I successfully contribute to the education that they deserved? It was a feeling of the estrangements of backgrounds and cultures, all waiting for me to utter my first words for the first time in their class room. I didn't come to Africa to westernize them. I was there in order for them to Africanize me. As little as they would realize it, it would be them from whom I would learn, far more than what they would learn from me.

"Good morning, Mista Holiday" It was Tandangu greeting me that next morning.

"Good Morning, Brother." I returned the greeting. "Tell me, where around here can I buy some rat poison?

Tandangu looked at me in surprise. "Uh, say what?"

"Rat poison. You know, stuff to kill rats, I've got to get rid of the rats in my house. They're everywhere,"

"Do you want to chop-um?" he asked.

"NO, I don't want to eat them I want to destroy them."

A few people in that part of Africa did eat rats. Tandangu caught on. "Oh, no sah." he exclaimed. "There is no rat poison sold here in this part of Africa."

"Well, why not?" I asked a bit impatiently.

He went on to explain: "You see, sah, if rat poison was sold at the market, somebody would buy all of it and use it for juju. He would just put it in somebody's mealy meal and kill him."

I just needed a little closure on the subject. "So you are telling me that the reason rat poison is not sold here is because somebody would use it as witchcraft to kill someone?

"Oh, yes." He answered.

After hearing this, it was difficult for me to come to a truce with my ignorance on the extremities of the methods of African witchcraft. Whether it was by snake bite or by rat poison, both were potent enough to twist a dying smile on your face. I was just an infant, lost in the great library called Africa.

CHAPTER 13

FIRST DAY IN CLASS

Mr. Ekoko, the Vice Headmaster, was waiting for Tandangu and me over by one of the class room blocks, which was located near the piggery. The piggery sounded off with the usual stench as it had begun to blossom, competing with the sun's intensity. The sun's hue painted Ekoko's face with an orange-red tinge. He stood proudly and as straight as a stalk of cane. Everything about him was intact, except for his wrinkled trousers which he wore noticeably too high exposing his ankles. He wore no socks, which was common in this part of Africa. In all, he was a neat little man who commanded the student's respect. The navy blue suit which he wore was tightly buttoned and hugged firmly about his chest. His neck tie which seemed to have choked him, hung short.

How he would survive the day's heat in one hundred and ten degrees would be a question that only he could have answered. He held firmly to the handle of his hippo cane, which was tucked beneath his arm.

Mild, smiling greetings were exchanged between us. "Mista Holiday," Ekoko began. "Since the Chief has accepted you to teach for us, the Headmistress and I have spent practically the entire night working out a syllabus and a time schedule for you. You will be teaching forms 1-A, 1-B, and 1-C History and English. However, your teaching English will be on a trial basis."

"A trial basis? Why is that?" I ask. He gave me no answer. It wasn't that I didn't know the answer, I was curious to hear what he had to say about it.

Ekoko continued. "You shall also teach forms 3-B and 3-C, Religious Knowledge. You will not focus on one particular religion. You will teach Comparative Religion." Then looking up with a smile, he ask, "How's that for a start?"

"Sounds pretty good to me" I replied. "But I am not so much in favor of teaching English on a trial basis. Especially when I was told that it was a required teaching for English speaking expats."

Ekoko ignored my point. "Good," He said. "Glad you have agreed. Now let me introduce you to the 3-C students. They range from ages fifteen to beyond twenty. Many of them had to enroll in school at their parent's convenience. Many of our students got a late start in life. For the 3-C students, this would normally be their History class. I will see to it that you get your text books right away."

We entered the class room. I was tense but tried not to show it. Chairs rumbled as the students immediately rose to their feet. All stood silently at attention. Only the lizard claws could be heard clamoring across the tin roof.

The students were beautiful to behold. All black, all in blue. Their faces were so diverse, so sun kissed, so unique, so promising, so African, so futuristic. As I looked at them, I was captured by their oneness, that solitary blackness of skin that dominated them. It was something to be desired, something to be envied, something equivalent to a man's dream of reaching out into the distant chasm of space to grasp a quasar and imprison it within his bosom. It was something like being given the privilege of standing before the God of all creation, the God who dispenses pigmentation and requesting from Him in the humblest way to be granted very deepest shade of ebony that infinity could afford. Something that would no doubt inspire the chuckle of angels when they would hear, "Please Lord, make me as black as you can."

My soul wanted to express things to the students that my tongue was not created to say.

"Good morning, students," the Vice Headmaster shouted.

"Goot ma-nin sah!"

"Let us now sing our National Anthem."

Ekoko raised up on the tips of his toes with an air of Victorian importance. He held up high his blood drawing hippo cane with the confidence of a seasoned conductor and led the students in singing the African National Anthem. As they began to sing, their voices became sweeter. My eyes watered. I could not restrain myself. I listened while they sang to the flag of black, red, and green: black that represented the color of their skin, red for the blood they spill to win back the green land that was already rightfully theirs. Eighty of them singing with such harmony.

They sang on: "Stand and sing of Africa proud and free, land of work and joy and liberty."

Their voices swelled and flooded the room. The employees outside of the class room could be seen standing at attention. For a few moments it seemed that their voices purified the air. It was inspiring just to know that here are a people who sing their National Anthem in their own country, every morning on a daily basis. They hold their country in the highest esteem. "Be seated" Ekoko ordered.

Again, the scraping of chairs, then complete silence. Then came the surprising introduction. "We have with us, a Negro."

"Wow," I said to myself. "Why did I not see that coming?" The students kept poker faces as though they were oblivious to the term.

"His name is Mista Holiday. He has come to us all the way from America. He has decided to settle with us in our country. He will be your teacher in history. Let us accept him by giving him a welcome to our country."

A shout returned with one voice, "Welcome to our country, Mista Holiday!" "And thank you in return, students." I replied.

I glanced about the poorly constructed class room. I noticed that the walls were made partly of mud bricks. Huge spiders dominated the rotten rafters. Termites perforated the supporting logs with tunnels. There were no black boards, only black paint sanded over of its gloss. The walls were so chipped that writing on them was difficult. The student's desk were splintered. I had to come to grips with the fact that I was not there to teach the walls, rafters, and desks rather, I was there to reconstruct the student's world view, sand down the splinters of their lives, and write on the black boards of their hearts the immutable truth about God. I was there to uncover at least some of the falsehoods that lie beneath the thin veneer of a fleeting human history that will someday collapse under the weight of Biblical Prophecy and shatter at the Feet of the Kingdom of God.

As lovely as the students were, it was still very obvious that they were victims of hardship. Undernourishment cried out in their faces.

A brief gaze out of the class room window and there strutted the tubby Chief, proudly headed toward the piggery. Following behind him were two of his worn out servants, pulling two carts sagging with palm wine and maize to slop his pigs.

Ekoko concluded his introduction: "You must pay careful attention to Mista Holiday. He has been to many places and has experienced many things. He has much knowledge to share. He no doubt knows more about Africa than any of us since he has visited many parts of the continent, traveling by land." With those words, he shook my hand and added "They are all yours sah."

He then walked out of the room.

Again, there was silence. All eyes were on me. I wished at the time that I had been a linguistic mechanic perhaps toting a linguistic toolbox. Then perhaps I could have reached out and picked up the word "Negro" that Ekoko had hurled across the room. I was quite sure that he meant no harm by using that phrase, but I felt uncomfortable with it.

A word that is not worth something is not worth using. Where are its nutrients? Its life-sustaining, its dignity, its values, its destiny?

The etymology of the word "negro" was first applied to certain universal human characteristics which meant to be stingy or sordidly parsimonious. The word found its way from there in to racial categories. It did not separate me from the students in my class. The word began with Africans and found slave status in America. How the word devolved from "Hametic" to "Negro," would require a separate history of its own and to describe the transition from the words "ulotrichous and sublime" to "nappy and subspecies," would no doubt require an undergraduate study. The word Negro is of Portuguese origin. In either case, the word was not intended by its so-called scholars to be a term of endearment. I am just as much a Hammite as was Melchisdeck, King of Salem, Priest of the Most High God (El Elyon). I was also set on course to teach a class of Hamites. Someday the name negro as will be all racial misnomers the world over for all people will be put to rest and it will not be over some one's dead body.

Black people should not just settle for what any man calls them. They are Hammetic people because they descended from Noah's second son, Ham. That title is of Hebrew origin but the ancestry of the black man far out dates their current classification. That is the term I accept. But neither

Noah or Ham nor his patriarch fathers were Hebrews.

As I stood before my students, I asked myself, "What is a 'Negro' supposed to do? Are the students to expect something from a Negro that they are not to expect from anyone else? My best? My worse? What about a black power salute? Or foot the Buzz, as Cab Callaway did it in the thirties. As another would make it famous in the eighties wearing a white glove?

We spend our lives chipping through the mine shafts of our own minds, chiseling away, separating the good thoughts from the stupid ones.

I began. "Students, since this is our first meeting, and seeing that most of our class period has already been taken, I thought it would be appropriate to spend the remainder of our time getting acquainted. You may share with me many things about your beautiful country and perhaps you would like to ask me some things about America."

After a brief second of silence, a hand went up from the back of the room.

"Yes, young man?"

"Sah, have you ever seen James Brown?" The girls giggled.

"No, I've seen a few celebrities but not the 'God father of soul. Another hand shot up.

"Sah, tell us, is what we see in the films about you people, true?"

I asked. "Things such as?"

The student rephrased the question, "What I mean, sah, is it true that the people in America move about with guns all the time?"

I answered, "Not everybody in America carry guns all the time, but our Constitution permits us to have the right to bear arms should we choose to do so. A special permit to carry a concealed firearm is required. You must remember that America has a history of guns and now has a gun culture. In America, criminals are outlawed from owning guns. The problem is that that particular law has weak enforcement. There are extreme delays and often time's deliberate procrastination within our judicial system which gives criminals the chance to repeat their acts of violence. Sometimes acts of terror are not dealt with speedily in the courts. They are often dragged on for years.

Some years ago, in America, the Chief Justice of the US Supreme Court, in an address said, 'The administration of the criminal law in this country is a disgrace to civilization. The trial of a criminal seems like a game of chance-- with all the chances in favor of the criminal. If he wins he seems to have the sympathy of a sporting public."

I then gave them an assignment.

"When you return to your quarters, turn in your Bibles to Ecclesiastes 8:11. "Because sentence against an evil work is not executed speedily, therefore the heart of the sons of men is fully set in them to do evil."

"Students, this you must never forget: When our biological development is not accompanied by spiritual growth, then the process of our development is incomplete. Without the constant grasp for spiritual maturity, we tend to become gullible, and if it is not hindered, we become intensely more depraved, totally incapable of reform, until finally we are nothing more than lummoxes roaming the earth in a subordinate state in desperate search for gratification. We then develop an insatiable lust that is far below animal level. We become void of sensitivity to the needs of others, which includes the sanctity of human life. What is the final outcome of a person like this?

"He becomes so degenerate that he is controlled by his own basic instincts. He is self-cannibalized. This accounts for why there are drive-by shootings and serial murders in America and mass slaughters in Africa."

For a few seconds there was silence, a surprising and deafening silence, a silence that brought back my memories of the apartheid nightmare I saw traveling through South Africa. A silence that reverberated with the screams and the terror of the blood bath they raged upon their black people. A silence that amplified the rage of the monstrous terror of Idi Amin in Uganda. I could hear the screams yet. The echoes were as clear as I wept uncontrollably and vomited until there was nothing else left when that day my nostrils breathed in the stench of those three hundred rotten corpses of Africa's beautiful black women. All had been lined up and machine gunned down by white South African soldiers.

"Students, you are the generation that will be responsible for ending atrocities in Africa," I commented. I couldn't bring myself to speak more about these things with these children not yet, at least. "I have time for one more question,"

"Sah, Why do blacks and whites in America hate each other?"

With a sigh, I responded. "This answer may take up

more time than we have, but let me say that not all blacks and white people in America hate each other.

Racism began in America when the first white in the American south decided that black skinned men were more suitable to work as slaves in the unbearable hot sun, to grow and harvest cotton. The Native American Indians simply refused to be slaves, although some of them did perform acts of servitude.

The next stage of racism was carried out when the first black man from Africa set foot on North American soil and was auctioned off to the highest bidder.

Later, after many years of slavery, there were a few white people in America who opposed the institution of slavery. They were called Abolitionist They fought for the freedom of black people and constructed the underground railroads. I believe that even today, the blood of those God-fearing abolitionist still runs through the veins of a few of their descendants.

"Personally, it is not in me to hate any man. I have many faults, but God spared me from that depravity. I tried once to hate a race of people, but I couldn't. However, there are traits identifiable in all cross cultures, including ours, that I truly can say I hate, and one of those are to despises the very existence of another race. The image of God is indiscriminate and the Breath of God is in every man's nostrils.

"When will the people in American learn this? When will the people in Africa and Asia learn this? They will learn it when they realize that we are not all worshiping the same God. A god that says for you to kill everybody that is not

in your religion cannot possibly be the same God who says
Thou shalt not kill."

"But, sah," ask a student Did not God in the Bible order
people to be killed?"

"Yes, He did, but for the most part, those whom He
ordered to be killed were counterfeit humans. They were
mimicking as humans, such as the Lion like men of Moab.
There is no resurrection for them. Isaiah 26:14 Dead, they
shall not live. Deceased, they shall not rise.

Either that or they humans that were too evil to repent.
I gave the students a practical example, reminding them
that right there within their classroom circles were students
among them with tribal differences and that they should try
to settle these before they graduate.

It was obvious that there were serious divisions among
the students and teachers as well. I saw it as a primitive,
undiluted form of inverted apartheid, the most heinous of
perfidies. For wherein does the hope lie when a man victim-
izes the people of his own race?

CHAPTER 14

PAPA BOUAMBOU

There was a senior gentleman living in a village not far from the college, with whom I had made an earlier acquaintance. He was affectionately called Papa Bouambou. He was cast into this paternal role for his wise counsel. His unquestionable demeanor was so commendable that in spite of his being childless, swarms of youngsters would gather nightly around his fire to listen to his yarns of yore. Papa had a tremendous sense of humor and would often remark, "I was perhaps the first African that had ever learned from an all-white African school."

"How so, Papa?" I ask. "You mean to say that you were actually admitted into the school?"

"Oh no! He would answer. "I merely sat outside beneath the classroom window and took notes. I stayed with that class until we graduated with honors."

Volleys of laughter burst out. Papa had rejected the offer of enlistment into the King's African Rifles. He felt that they would eventually become an elite force that would someday intimidate his people.

He did, however, work under colonial rule as an assistant overseer as an interpreter within a cola plantation. During the entirety of our conversations, Papa had never expressed any resentment toward the British colonizers. He decided that perhaps it would be better that he should profit by their positive views about nation building, and other ideas that would be beneficial to Africans.

"It is the French rule in Africa that I was so much against." He would say. "The French are more arrogant than the British. Their influence over certain Africans is self-destructive. so many of our politicians have identified with their ways."I had decided one day to pay Papa a visit. I had some questions about Chief Omubu that I needed answers to. Since Papa was native born in the area and had so much history to share, who would be in a better position to provide for me what I was seeking?

My journey that morning began about 7:00. As I was approaching Papa's village, something spectacular caught my attention. Directly within my path, a solitary eagle swooped suddenly down from out of the azure African sky, and like some avian warrior, hurled a penetrating, uncanny shriek of victory as he plunged his spear-like talons into the writhing sides of a deadly cobra. Then as swiftly as he had appeared, he spiraled his broad wings upward again toward the skies, brushing the straw-thatched roofs of the village of Kamba, grasping in those powerful claws his dangling pretzel twisted trophy as it struggled in vain to free itself. We travelers below gasped in awe as we watched with open mouths and pointing fingers. The eagle, our hero of the day, vanished out of sight, back into the womb of the emblazoned sky.

When Papa Bouambou heard of my awesome experience, he leaped with joy and thanked God that the eagle was there to save my life. "This, my son, is a fitting signal that tells of the victories and defeats that you will encounter here in Africa."

It was late into the evening and just after dark before Papa and I were able to sit by the fire outside of his hut to talk. We had spent the entire day gathering wood and planting vegetable seeds. He was actually teaching me the skills of communal life. These lessons would be desperately needed in the event that my salary would somehow come up short.

That night as Papa and I sat by the fire, I brought up the subject of Chief Omubu. Before Papa began his story, he slowly stroked his tired, chapped legs and then his arms with some chopped up coconuts which he had boiled to get oil. His oiled limbs gleaming in the fire light caused him to resemble a knight in shining armor.

"He is a wounded lion, my son." He said as he motioned for me to fetch a couple of logs for the fire. He carefully placed one of the logs in the flames.

"The Chief is a wounded lion. Ever since he was kicked out of the Parliament some years ago, it appears that things have not set right with him. He has completely changed."

Although I had heard about that event, I was careful not to speak out of turn. There was much more to learn from this story and I didn't want to miss a word of it.

"The Chief was appointed from right out of the bush and given a seat in the National Assembly, a big mistake our Government made." Papa stressed with extended arms. He paused and sat his bowl of oil on a stump next to him and continued.

"At first, it wasn't because of his brilliance that he was appointed. Being the son of a Chief was why they accepted him. Then again, the Parliament has a policy that no tribe in our country should be without representation. The Chief's tribe is one of the most backward in the country."

Papa grabbed the other log and tossed it on the fire. The sparks ascended in spirals like tiny souls being freed from the torments of earth, summonsing the nearby fire flies to escort them on their way.

"My son," Papa continued. "There is a river in our country called the Mongu. On the other side of it the people speak French. They are called Francophones. Their way of life is far different from ours. Just think of it as a liquid Berlin wall. The years of colonization by two nations has divided us and effected our cultures. The Francophone way of life is far different from ours. They've a tendency to live very extravagant. The seat of our government is in that Francophone world. The life style on that side of the Mongu was just too much for the Chief. "

Somewhere in the blackness a bush baby began screaming, causing that same deafening vibration. Papa waited until it was finished, then continued.

"Now, can you imagine taking a man out of the bush and sticking him right into a society whose lifestyles are extravagant? The Chief nearly went mad. He spent money faster than a kudu could run from a lion and the women. Oh, let me tell you! Between the both of them, champagne flowed like rivers. He had women waiting for him right outside on the very Parliament steps. They were even heard to call him 'Chiefy.' Can you imagine? Chiefy!

Papa leaned forward and applied a bit of oil to his knees. It was about that time that we could hear hyenas in the distance, battling it out with a few village mongrels. "Every night, without fail, those worrisome animals," he muttered. Then he added, "But, this is Africa."

Before Papa could continue with his discussion, he was approached by a young man carrying a sack containing a goliath rat that he was trying to sell. The animal's body was covered with large orange body lice. They darted in and out of its hair.

"Aren't you the boy whom I turned down a few days ago?" Papa ask.

"Yisah" the man answered.

"What is wrong with you, man? Did I not tell you that I don't eat rats?"

"You did, sah," He answered nervously.

"Well, what makes you think that my appetite has changed overnight? I do not eat rats, do you understand? I can never put something in my mouth that you can never kill. If you eat a rat, chew it up, and swallow it, the damn thing will just reassemble back together in your stomach and when you use the outhouse, you will just give birth to the same rat.

"Now, I am telling you this for the last time, do not return to my hut again with another one of those dam rats. Have I made myself clear?"

"Yisah" said the man and trotted off into the night.

Papa continued. "Now, where was I? Oh yes, the Chief. It was when he realized how much authority he had been given that he changed for the worse. He thrives now on the hinges of treachery. When you return to the college, just look about you." Papa demonstrated by waving his walking stick.

"Most of his opulence, I suppose you could call it his house, his college, his palm plantation, and all those animals, especially his piggery were all gotten by bribery, extortion and stealing from the students and the teachers. His deeds in the Parliament caught up with him when he somehow misappropriated about fifty million francs of our government 's funds.

"Somehow, after a long investigation, no one could find any evidence against the Chief. All the same, he was eventually escorted out of the parliament. When he got out on the Parliament steps, he turned and cursed them from the President to the very gendarmerie that guarded the Parliament building.

"He swore that he would put a curse on them that they would never be able to shake. The Parliament took it seriously. No one in our country makes light of threats or curses. They suspected that he might return some day with a subsidized group of rebels and stage a Coup de tat. They decided not to pursue the matter any further, leave well enough alone, and perhaps matters would just die out. As it stands now, there are no real friends in the Chief's life. There are only real enemies, and that happens to be everybody. To him all men are useable and capable of being manipulated."

There was one question more concerning the Chief about which I had to have an answer. It was regarding the strange attachment that he had for his pigs. What was so captivating about them that harnessed his emotions to callous extremes that held such a cryptic sway over him, so mesmerizing that even the cry of an infant could not awaken pity? A callousness that ignored his family, the students, the teachers and his workers? The little ones in his village perished from a deadly measles virus before his dry eyes. Who, but him would flood his pig's trough with flagons of wine and sing to them the melodies of endearment which were worthy only of humans, and swore to those creatures that the very aroma of their urine held the eternal fragrance of the gods?

Papa Bouambou provided some of my answers.

"It all began when the Chief was a little boy" He said. "His grandmother came into their village one day carrying a small pig. No one knows where she got it. Some claim that she found it tied up in the forest. She was deeply involved in witchcraft. She gave the animal to the Chief, also named Victor, at that time, a young prince. She told him that the pig held great powers and that it was connected to spirits that would bring him great wealth. His grandmother instructed him to watch it carefully, feed it well, and never forget to flood it with libations of wine."

Papa, like many seniors, puffed on his pipe with marijuana. It grows to the height of trees in Africa and is perhaps the most potent in the world. It was not illegal and nobody seem to make any issue about it. Papa continued while stuffing his pipe.

"There were some youngsters that were up to mischief that came from a nearby village. Their plot was to steal young Victor's pig, take it into the forest and slaughter it, which they did. When Victor found his pig, it was completely mutilated. He was so angry that he begged his grandmother to put a curse on the boys, which she did.

"It was over a spread of weeks that the boys were all found dead from cobra bites. Each night, when a boy entered his huts, he would be attacked by a spitting cobra. It would somehow crawl into their mats. As I said, this occurred over a spread of weeks, I suppose to keep from drawing too much suspicion, if that was possible. Whether or not their deaths were actually caused by witchcraft, no one can really say, but here in Africa, everyone takes witchcraft seriously.

"From that time forward, the Chief has acted very strange toward other people. He trusts no one."

CHAPTER 15

DEMONS AMONG THE FLOWERS

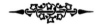

It began as a very promising morning. The Form Four Class had assembled for the Comparative Religions studies. The National anthem was sung. No sooner had the students seated, than an eager hand went up with a question. She was Beauty Tamatu, an Ibo girl and an outstanding student.

"Sah," she addressed me with a wide smile. "Although I believe it, I am having some difficulty reconciling the origin of matter within the Biblical Creation account. Can you help me out?"

"Yes, Beauty," I responded. "You have already given your solution when you stated that you 'believe.' It is not a matter of proof, but a matter of belief, which is the key to accepting the Bible's account for the existence of matter."

I asked the class to open their Bibles to the Book of Hebrews, 11:3 where it states that it is "By faith that we understand that the heavens were created through the spoken word of God."

It was at this time that I had decided to light a spark to their inquisitive minds. "Before we discuss the presence of matter in space, how do you account for the existence of space itself?"

I paused, looking around the room. All was quiet. The students were no doubt searched as well for an answer.

I continued "How many of us have ever given thought about the origin of space? I ask you this question, class, because to me, the existence of space is more mysterious than the objects that are floating around in it. Now may I ask you again, how do you account for it? Where did it come from, and what is it other than mere extension? Even if a man believed in a big bang, it would not give an account for the space that it occurred in."

"But, sah," responded Beauty. "Why can't we just say that space is nothing?"

"The reason that it is impossible to conclude that space is simply nothing, is because space has attributes." I answered.

"It has allow-ability. Objects are allowed to exist in it and move through it. It also has stability. It is always there. If the earth should vanish, it would have no effect on space. So how could we possibly call anything that has characteristics, nothing? Has it ever occurred to you that God, who created space, can also see it, knows what it looks like and has created boundaries for it?"

Eyes lit up. I continued.

"Since God is not confined to either space or time, would you believe me if I were to tell you that there is as much of God inside of a tiny thimble as there is of Him in the entirety of the universe? ...and as far as He is concern, within His being, there is no center nor circumference?"

Charity Anuga, a Bamenda girl, sat about midway in the class. "So let us hear what Charity has to say about what we have just discussed." I pointed to her. "Charity? Let's hear your point of view."

Charity sat silent. I called her again, but got no response. She merely sat quietly, starring out of the window. This was the moment that I was to have an encounter with the unexpected. I walked over to Charity to get a closer look. There was a strange, watery glare in her eyes. A heavy silence fell over the class. Every one there was aware of what was happening except me.

I touched her forehead with the back of my hand. There was no response. She was perspiring heavily, but strangely enough, she was ice cold. I waved my hand in front of her face. She wasn't fazed. Suddenly, she gazed down at her own body as if she had just inhabited it. The students held their breath as they watched her. They were gripped by an uncanny fear.

"What is the matter with Charity?" I asked.

"She has evil spirits sah," came a girl's nervous reply from across the room. Suddenly, it was as if someone had called her. Charity slowly stood up and started out the door. Several of the girls ran after her.

"Where are you all going?" I asked.

"We must catch her sah! If we don't, she'll run into the bush and hurt herself!"

There was a story in the Bible like this where a broken-hearted father plead with Yeshua to exorcise his son. "And oft times it hath cast him into the fire and into the waters, to destroy him."

"All right. Go quickly and catch her,"

I turned to the students who remained in the class.

"Does this happen quite often around here?" I asked.

"Yissah" They responded.

"There are plenty of students here with evil spirits," another answered.

"But what happened in Charity's case?"

"She was told not to eat or help kill a chicken, sah," one girl answered.

"Who told her not to?"

"The spirits, sah."

"Did she help kill one?" I asked.

The girl hesitated, then went on to explain. "Well, yes, but not exactly sah. She was helping her club to pick the feathers from one which someone else had killed, but it was just the same as her killing one."

"But what has that to do with her having evil spirits?" I asked.

"She just fagot, sah." exclaimed another girl.

"*My goodness!*" I thought. "*How on earth could she possibly for get something like that?*"

"Well, class, tell me. What happens to her next?"

"What do you mean, sah?" one asked.

"I mean how will she get rid of it? How is she cured?"

"Oh, her friends in the dorm will know what to do. If they can't help her, one of them will go to her village or to the bush and find some African medicine."

"But why doesn't she just go to the clinic?"

"Oh, no sah she can't do that."

"Why can't she?"

"Because she can even die if she does. The spirits will become very annoyed. Only African medicine can help her."

"Whenever matters about the Divine are being discussed, it is more than likely that an uncomfortable demonic presence will manifest itself, if nothing more than a "What are you guys talking about?"

I learned a lot from similar experiences like the one that Charity had, of how she was tortured by demons and how it affected everybody around her. The students were right. The entire college was under demonic inspiration, beginning with the Chief. For the duration of our lives, we will always be confronted by the three contagious races the angelic, the human, and the demonic. Not for one second will we ever in our mortal life retire from their intrusive involvement. They are always contending for the mastery over our puny existence. It is their cosmic struggle against each other for the total theater of man's heart. Demons are in a perpetual state of anger. They often exult in a man with pretensions of happiness, but their portentous designs are fossilized within an immutable state of eternal hatred. Evil entities are working tirelessly in behalf of our worst interest and the human race will never have the well wishes of hell.

Mankind is a victim that is caught up in a maniacal rage that is hell bent on his total destruction.

A university student does not have to fly to Africa to do research to write a thesis on demonism. He can do extensive work on its activities and evils right in the streets and inside of the skyscrapers of America. He can write a dissertation about one single night club alone as a matter of fact, he could do a graduate study within the very jungles of his own college campus or knock on the doors of the Shamans that occupy the dormitories of his beloved Alma Mater and study the characteristics of his atheistic colleagues, and it would earn for him a PhD in "selective ignorance." But before he does, he must be cautioned that it is a dangerous thing to attempt to experiment with God.

A student once ask me, "Sah, do you have spirits?"

My reply to her was, "Yes, I have two spirits. One is my own that I was born with, and the other I received when I was born again. That is God's Holy Spirit."

Africa has a spiritual burden, which she has carried for centuries. She is also known for the rarest of flowers. The most beautiful of those are her women, but many of those are being plucked by demons, and as soon as they have withered, they are cast to the side of the road.

America too has beautiful flowers that are snapped off their stems out of the gardens of families, societies, schools, and churches. These delicate blossoms are pollinated with cocaine dust by demon bees whose hives are hidden in the most unbelievable places, operated by the merchants of Satan. When these flowers have lost their attractiveness, they too, like the flowers of Africa, are cast onto the streets.

They are beautiful human flowers that we must guard, we must water and we must protect. Why? Because we cannot live without them.

CHAPTER 16

MONKEY ON THE MENU

"The Chief wishes to see me now, right now, at this time of the night? You have got to be kidding," I grumbled as my arms shot out franticly. It was as if I had expected the tired messenger to materialize some visible piece of logic that would be acceptable enough to calm my frustrations.

"Yisah, now, now," came the hurried reply.

"The *Chief has to be up to something*". I thought as I stepped out into the darkness, locking the hut's door behind me. It had to be something out of the ordinary.

We drove in the messenger's car. By this time the Chief had become so repelling toward the others it was as though he hemorrhaged discontent. The staff, also by their demeanor, obviously hated him. They responded only to his commands, nothing more, and whenever possible, they barely responded at all. The staff's resentment was justifiable. They felt cheated and robbed, and they had been. The students loathed him as well. To them, he was a "father gone renegade," an exploiter of both them and their parents. They accused him of slave labor.

Considering the long distances that the students lived from the school some of them as far as two or three days travel they couldn't just run home, grab a meal and return to classes. The Self-Reliant Projects were theirs by right. They labored hard at keeping up, but were denied the projects' bounty by the Chief. Again, the teachers were hoping for some type of coup that would force a government takeover, regularize salaries, and nationalize the school. Most of them would have preferred to have the Headmistress initiate the rebellion. Perhaps the outcome of all this would restore the sanity needed to mandate an academic environment.

The African night was rude and uninviting. If the pitch blackness had the weight of its thickness, it would have mercilessly descended, grinding me to powder. There was nothing about it but uncertainty. It dared me to step out of the comfort of the messenger's car, and I reluctantly accepted its challenge. The frogs and insects never let up. They amplified their melancholy sounds with mournful eulogies that lamented the deaths of their fellows that perished during the day. Their noises were so loud, so exaggerated, that it nearly deafened the pounding of the distant drums. It was only when I was compelled to stare up at the glittering stars that I could feel some hope of promise. Although they could provide no light for me on the ground, they served as simple reminders that if only I would be patient and ponder, I would someday escape through their brilliant corridors and rest, at last, at the Feet of God.

As I got out of the car, the pungent odor of urine was a cautioning reminder of my first visit there. At the back of the compound, a generator rattled. That too, was a luxury that the school did not have. To my relief, Whiskey and Bombo, the Chief's mongrels, were out in the night defending their territory with snarling disputes and insanities that were mingled with the unearthly screams of the hyenas. They and their grueling fights could be heard. It was all an uncanny reminder to me of the night that I spent in the southern desert village of Ethiopia months earlier.

During the entire time, I struggled desperately to keep the village dogs and their enemy hyenas from breaking down my hut door as they fought each other to the death. Their growling, the hyena's laughter and the pitiful yelping were mingled with indescribable terror. God's creatures which should never have met in the first place, were engaged in horrifying mortal combat, until finally, the next morning, before sunrise, the hyenas retreated, limping back to the hills. I slowly opened my hut door and there on the ground in front of me stood puddles of blood, ripped off patches of hair, bits of flesh, and weary dogs licking their wounds.

What a sacrifice for their loyalty as they guarded their pups and a village that could scarcely feed themselves, let alone their dogs.

Tonight the Chief's parlor was dimly lighted when the driver and I entered. From my first impression, from what I could see the inside stood in stark contrast to the outside of the house. It was also unbelievable that such lavish taste could be acquired by a man and embellished beyond what should have been his most precious possessions, his very own children, and in contrast to that, he cared more for his swine with religious affection. If his children were of no concern to him, then why even bother to mention the teachers and the students? And to think that this very man, who was behind it all, would stop at nothing until everyone around him was bound and cast into the dungeon of his depraved mind.

The house had many rooms. I would not get to see them all but what I saw was enough. I stepped onto a powdery red plush carpet that covered the length of the floor. There were carved mask and statues of ebony that graced the corners of the room. A large book shelf and a china cabinet were used for displaying pottery and expensive carvings. Instruments of witch craft hung on the walls and over the doors. Omens of caution spoke a language to intruders that only a country man could understand and by all means, take heed not to infringe upon. Broad back matching chairs of ebony, all carved to the minutest detail were positioned around most beautiful coffee table. I was awed by its depiction of the various phases of African life inscribed with mallet and chisel: hunters returning to the village with antelopes swinging from poles women pounding fufu, warriors in battle, wine tapers in palm trees, midwives delivering babies, celebrations and festivities showing drummers and dancers, all murals of carved mastery. I was later informed that this exquisite work had been accomplished by a Mr. Martin Taku, a local carver, and that he had received far less than what he had ask the Chief for his labor.

Being in the company of parliament ministers for quite some time, had taught the Chief about how a house could look. It was the magnetism of the French contagion of luxury that the Francophone African elitist admired. They spoke French and often vacationed in France.

The driver quietly beckoned for me to enter the dining room where there was a soothing glow of candle light. I did not see the Chief at first. I could have sworn that he was not present in the room. I did notice in the front of me, hanging on the wall in full spread, a fourteen foot python skin. While I was exploring, a voice startled me.

"I ate dat python four months ago, Mista Holiday."

I turned, and there behind me alone, at the head of a loaded table, beneath a tinkling chandelier, sat Chief Omubu. "I caught it myself. He said." I learn the skill of killing pythons when I was a boy. My Father told me that if I was to become a man, I would have to kill a very large python and bring it home for everybody to eat. I still eat them. I will eat anything, forest meat, bush meat. I even eat monkey."

There it was lying on the table along with practically everything that a forest gourmet could possibly crave a monkey that resembled a roasted infant with tiny hands clenched.

"I even eat dey head," He said, holding it out, offering it to me. "Sit down, Mista Holiday," he added. "Do you eat monkey? Monkey is good." He laughed. He had gotten a kick out of the frown which I tried not to show.

"No, Chief," I answered. "I'm not ready for monkey."

The Chief shook his stubby finger at me.

"You, Holiday, you have too much European in you. Ah, but you take my word for it, you will eat monkey before you leave our Africa!" I sat watching the Chief in amazement as he sat gorging his self. There was more than enough to choose from. It was a lengthy table glowing with candles, and I was sitting at the other end of it.

The Chief savagely tore in half a loaf of bread and extended half of it to me. I took it, trying not to be meticulous. I glanced at it, trying to conceal that I could see the grease from his fingers that smeared its crust. Somehow I would have to become accustomed to Africa's eating habits. Most of the meals are shared out of the same bowl. Every one eats with their fingers, and even hands are washed in the same bowl of water.

The Chief plunged his hand into a bowl of hot garri, rolled it into a neat golf ball and sent it hurling down his guzzler. That was washed down by a large gulp of wine, sanctioned with an unscrupulous belch. After stripping a chicken leg, he proceeded to talk with jaws bulging. He had a very pronounced accent and I had difficulty making out exactly what it was that he was saying, but now that he had his mouth so full, it was impossible. Had it not been for his pointing at the table, I would not have understood him to say, "Eat, Mesah Holiday, eat!"

I often used Bible verses to guide me through those trying experiences often encountered in Africa and I must confess that I was not always obedient to them. Whenever

I did not bother to listen, hardship would soon follow and they were often so severe that only God Himself could save me.

As I sat at the Chief's table, I remembered the admonishment from Proverbs 23:1-3. "When thou sittest to eat with a ruler, consider diligently what is before thee: And put a knife to thy throat, if thou be a man given to appetite. Be not desirous of his dainties for they are deceitful meat."

The meat is the trap that appeals to the lower appetite. Words of deceit are magnetic appeals to the higher cravings. The Chief was indeed a ruler and of course there were dainties on his table that all the hallucinogens on the planet could not entice me to be desirous of, but there were far more subtle things to be very cautious about. One of them was to be sure not to allow my eyes to become fixed on what the table held. Another heads up was that I should eat with my ears and not so much with my mouth. Listen carefully for flattery. How can anyone flatter you who doesn't really know you? And if he does think that he knows you, then you should be all the more suspicious of him, because he can never know more about you than you do not know about yourself. What man is it on this earth that has fully explored the infinity of his own universe?"

I sat silent at the Chief's table and he ate while I watched. Until he had finished his meal, he had very little to say. In Africa it is usually that way. You speak to a Chief after he has spoken to you. I was like an invisible man in his presence. You never interfere with a man when he is engaged in worship. The Chief's table was his shrine, his stomach was his god and for those few moments he was in the solemn act of worship. He lived to eat while those of us who were in the grasp of his power only ate to live. He had sacrificed his conscience on the altar of apathy. He had cremated any compassion that he might have had. He had hurled his self into the center of the lowest sphere where there exist no direction, neither up nor down. The only alternative left was to self-destruct.

The Chief was King of the Swine and he lived by their code "I will eat as much as I can eat while I am standing. When I can stand no longer from the weight of my food, I will lie down and eat. I will stop eating as long as I am asleep, and even then I will dream of eating until I am awake. Only when the slop ceases to fall on my head, then and then only will I gaze into the heavens for more."

Before the Chief explained why he had sent for me, he consumed his last morsel and downed a glass of wine. He sent a loud, unabashed belch across the table at me. I could literally see its heat wave as it came and released its sickening stench of monkey, fufu, garri, boiled eggs and wine. I have always been overly sensitive toward bad odors. I must admit that at times my imagination gets the best of me. There are some things that I don't bother to comment on, but when things are quite out of the ordinary, I will often make mention of them especially when that something is potent enough to make history, then history should be recorded.

"Mista Holiday" began the Chief. "I have decided to appoint you as administrator and General Manager of my college."

An uneasy feeling gripped my stomach as I sat listening. "Tomorrow I will have the Headmistress to deliver the statement to you officially in writing with my signature and stamp."

CHAPTER 17

THE RELUCTANT
PROMOTION

The Chief showed little emotion two days later after I had informed him of my willingness to take the position. In fact his pride was lacerated when I hesitated to jump at his orders. I had no idea of what I had gotten myself into. As far the Chief was concern, had he the slightest premonition about the problems that I would be facing in this new venture, he would never have had the audacity to give me a warning in advance. I knew that I was between a rock and a hard place. To reject the Chief's offer would have brought on nothing but uncertainty for me. My well being would have hung in the balance. It would certainly infuriate the Headmistress, not to mention my colleagues. I had to face them every day. They would have known that the Chief and I had met behind their backs. As far as the students were concern, they were willing to believe anything that the Headmistress and the teachers would drill into their heads about me.

They were pivotal enough to be turned into a force to be reckoned with. They were not merely students, but also a combination of tenants and farm workers. They had access to machetes, and were skilled in using them. There were also other means at their disposal, such as pitch forks and kerosene. These were their everyday tools used for self-reliance. They were motivated for anarchy. Their motivation was also charged with an insoluble rhetoric that they had learned from the volunteers who came to their college from China.

The volunteers taught the students a course in acupuncture while also giving them immunization shots against measles. But, as nothing is free, the Chinese ulterior motive was to promote Communist ideology. Every student was given a copy of Chairman Mao's Little Red Book. The effectiveness was demonstrated in their choice of words, such as imperialism the proletariat, and paper tiger

Oddly enough, although it may have sounded amusing to them, they were not content with the Chairman's solution to sever hunger while engaged in revolutionary warfare: "Rather than surrender to starvation, take off leather belts, shoes, and wallets, and boil and eat them."

Mrs. Diop, until now, had done no evil. There might have been times when she might have insinuated in some of her remarks during a heat of passion that could have incited a Decembrist outburst on the part of the students, but if the students and teachers were that attached to her, as bossy as she was, then there was no room for anyone else to complain.

I had to admit that she treated me with fairness. I didn't

always agree with her methods of discipline. But she had grown weary in her struggles with the Chief. Had he not stood in her way, perhaps she would have carried the school to higher levels. Her frustrations were understandable, and she certainly did not get the credit that she deserved for her tenacious influence at the school.

There was a textbook in the school's syllabus. It was *Animal Farm* by George Orwell. The Headmistress decided that she would teach the class. It would be used later as the bible that would inspire a clever ploy. It had all of the subversive ingredients delectable enough to incite a revolution. This was the story that gave some clarity to the Headmistress's obvious intentions.

In the fable, it was Farmer Jones who had been driven from the Manor Farm by his disgruntled animals. Old Major, the prize boar, was the inciter of this uprising just before he died, and right after making his speech. It was brought to the animals attention that Mr. Jones had them working harder while they ate less. There were other pigs such as Snow Ball, Squealer and finally Napoleon, along with fellow pigs and other animals that succeeded in accomplishing a successful revolution. But in the end, it was the pigs that wallowed in luxury and had drank all of the whiskey. The other animals did not see where the revolution caused them to be any better off. In the end, they destroyed the pigs.

She was irate. In fact, I had never seen the Headmistress so infuriated as she was on the day of the so called official handing over. The decision that was made behind closed doors was about to be made public, and to her embarrassment.

I never wanted it to be this way. I had always kept myself out of the conniving business. There are people who live by that code and are pretty skilled at it but eventually it will catch up with them. It's all about the law of Seed Time and Harvest, sowing and reaping, the immutable law of Full Circle. Sowing may be seen as sweet and enjoyable, but reaping can sometimes be a batch of detestable conglomerations.

"Here, Mr. Holiday here are your keys." She grumbled as she took them from her desk drawer. "I suppose I should be relieved to hand these over to you, but I should have been there when all of this was decided. I wasn't informed of this until just yesterday," she sighed, then commented "Mr. Holiday, I can't say that I congratulate you on your promotion. It's not a real promotion. It's a set up. "But," she hesitated, "I suppose I will assist you with anything that I can. You just beware the Chief will use you in any way that he can. He sees others as mere animals. It's as if he is the only bipedal one among us. He even treats his pigs as if they walked on two legs." Diop cautioned me again, "Mr. Holiday, you best be careful."

"Be careful?" I asked.

"Oh," she said, "You'll learn soon enough. By the time the Chief finishes starving you around here, creating a labyrinth for you, inveigling you into a web of lies, making it impossible for you to pay his bills, the college's bills and yours, and besides all that, he will blame you to the public for all of the short comings here at the college."

I somehow believed what the Headmistress had told me but I was willing to take my chances anyway. The whole idea of coming to Africa was taking a chance. Passing through Rwanda just after the slaughter was taking a chance. Being held at gun point at the Tanzanian border was taking a chance. Passing between villages quarantined because of the highly contagious green monkey virus was taking a chance. Staggering beneath the hot sun with no weapon in Zambia's lion country and listening to them roar just on the other side of the hill was taking a chance. But I took them and I can only comment that had it not been for the face of God, any one of those chances would have been my last.

Mrs. Diop and my values were not too far estranged. She was certainly not a racist to say the least. Neither was I. For some reason, I find it impossible to hate. Racism creates hate and when mixed with values, you come up with hypocrisy. Why it is that a man who hates will often admit to it, but that same man will resent being labeled a hypocrite?

The Headmistress recognized that she had also been victimized. The difference between she and I was that she had the power and tools to do something about it. At the slightest suggestion, she was capable of persuading any one in the compound to carry out her wishes. She could shout at them, call them idiots and often used other invective that objectified humiliating descriptions but all who were concern seemed impervious. They simply walked away scratching their heads. She was still, in spite of it all, their mother away from home as I said earlier.

I had concluded that if a man should label a man of a different ethnicity an idiot, it wouldn't necessary make him a racist. In all probability the other person may well be an idiot. The problem lies in one's blind boldness to assume the unauthorized authority to make an assessment of one who was created in the image of God. Should a man see another as an idiot simply because he did not meet arbitrary standards? Could the chance be that he in his renowned wisdom to make such a diagnosis, he may actually be replacing his protagonist as a prototype?

CHAPTER 18

FIRE OF THE MOTHER HEN

Mrs. Diop was irate. For the past few months she had been pulling her hair out, so to speak, in a desperate attempt to keep the students from "losing it, going berserk or perhaps abandoning the school altogether and returning to their homes. In fact, the situation at the school was so strenuous that she actually did grant permission to the minority of youngsters that lived nearby to return to their huts. Murder was now in her eyes. She could not restrain her feelings any longer. Enough was enough!

The Head Prefect had handed her a letter that the students had written to the Chief. They had requested that she would be the one to hand it to him. Mrs. Diop had read the letter and had decided that she would not change a word of it, since it described exactly the way that they felt.

"That's it," she shouted, slamming her pencil on her desk so hard that it snapped. "That's it!" she repeated, holding up the remaining piece. "I will break him just as I did this pencil. This is the last straw I'm going to give that Chief a piece of my mind."

The faithful trio Ekoko, Tandangu, and Eta spoke softly to her as they tried their best to persuade her to see it their way.

"Please, Madame, we beg of you, try not to get yourself all worked up. Is it really worth it? Give it some time at least wait until after you have given it some thought. "

"That is exactly what I have been doing for the past two years," she said. "Thinking, thinking, thinking and you know what, boys? As dubious as it may sound, I am tired of thinking. It's time for action!"

Tandangu spoke out. "Madame, we all know that Chief Omubu is a very dangerous man treacherous in fact. We have no idea of what he is capable of, or what he will do to you. Especially you, a woman challenging him to his face. Oh, Madame, this is not good, not good at all."

"I can appreciate your concern, boys. Diop answered. "But leave the results to me. I've had it up to here with that Chief and his shenanigans."

She zipped her finger across her throat. "This, this crap has got to stop!"

Diop brushed hastily passed the men. She paused at the door and frowned. "The one thing that I will regret will be inhaling the stench from those filthy pigs and watching those blue bottle flies zinging all about the place. How it is that a person can get a charge out of smelling pig bowels is a mystery to me."

When Diop left her office, a crowd of students cleared

a path for her. They were aware that she had read their letter. They saw it in her hand and in her eyes as she passed through their midst. A few of them followed her. Tension was in the air. They could feel it. What would it be like to see two officials having it out? Even better, what would it be like to see a confrontation between a "peeled one" and a black man?

African children described white men as the peeled ones. They mean no offense by it but merely use the term as a colloquial between a peeled potato and one that is not, as Tabby had said.

To the students, the Headmistress was a twenty-first century Joan of Arc, a valiant bag of ticked off cats. Even then, she appeared as though she was ready for a scuffle. Her blond hair was disheveled, glowing in contrast to her face, which redden with each step she took. She was a blue eyed hell cat, fixated on the direction of the pig pen. As it is often said, "Hell hath no fury like a woman's scorn," and now this woman was scorned.

As soon as Diop saw the Chief, she walked right up to him, stared directly into his eyes, and came out with a blast.

"Chief, I want a word with you!" She roared.

The Chief was startled, but remained silent. It was as if he already knew that he had it coming. But this was something new. It wasn't customary for a woman to approach a Chief in the manner which she did. She was suppose to walk quietly, humbly and then kneel in front of him. Bringing a bowl of fruit would have been impressive. If she had been an elderly woman, just bowing would have been appropriate, and by all means, she should avoid making direct eye contact with him.

But Diop was different. She neither bowed nor kneeled. For the Chief to gaze into those blue, piercing eyes, those no nonsense pair of Scottish eyes that had no smiles to offer, was something that was never expected nor codified within the traditions of African Chief protocol.

The African heat was intense, but the temper that flared between the Chief and the Headmistress was a heat that could blush the sun. Mrs. Diop was in such an emotional state of anger that she could barely squeeze out another word. Before she could express herself any further, she began to choke up. Then came the rain that is, the tears. There is hardly a man on this earth that can ignore the cry of a baby or resist giving in to the tears of woman. Rather than to see her weep, a man will rob a bank, work three jobs or walk to the far ends of the earth in his quest to bring her the desires of her heart. Rather than to see a single drop of that briny liquid trickle down her darling face, he would renounce his pride and beg on his knees in the teeming streets for a single rose to dry her tears. He would gladly cast his self into the role of a beggar by day as long as he could be her lover by night that he might drink her tears and quench his thirst until the very last drop falls from her chin, for it is there where he is nearest to her lips.

It was not so with the Chief. He was tear proof. Only the squeal of a pig could soften his heart.

The Headmistress quickly recovered from her sullen burst of tears. She was not in the least the "tough ole gal" that she often let on to be. Beneath that facade of exaggerated invective lay a heart of gold-plated compassion. She certainly had not wept in an effort to stir the Chief's conscience for it had plead with him until it had contracted laryngitis. Hers were the tears of a desperate mother, a mother hen brooding over her chicks. She was that hen who violated the laws of aerial dynamics and flew to the top of a hut to rescue her chick from the clutches of a hawk. She followed the instincts of a Headmistress locked into the dilemma of a sinking ship, as she tried to rescue her teachers and students. Her reputation was the least of her concerns.

For the Chief to see her weep was of course a victory for him. For her to break down in his presence spoke volumes to his self-deceived ego. He had defeated his greatest enemy. He was the new Shaka Zulu. Shaka once had one of his wives shoved into a hut with a starving hyena. Chief Omubu would stylize his victory as throwing the Headmistress to his glutton pigs or at least it would be his biggest fantasy. To him it was a point well proven.

The Chief was a heretic to the moral laws of Africa, to mankind, to nature, to the world. He was confident that from this time forward, and for the duration of eternity, he could hop across the starry lily pads of the universe usurping authority from the angels and reclining on their sapphire thrones with pigs as his sentinels. He had proven that any time he decided, he could quash his conscience at the expense of other men's miseries. Far worse, he had acquired an insatiable addiction to keep on trying to prove it.

At this juncture, it was not the Chief's ignorance about

his self that was to bring him to inevitable doom. It was the true arch villain, his blindness the lack of insight into women where most men fail. It was this very oversight that would prove to be the terror of his life. He should have learned this lesson from his pigs "It is the Sow that always gets what she wants."

The Chief knew nothing about the spiritual dynamics of a woman. She was created out of fire (Isha). She also has within her a life sustaining water. She may be as heavenly as an angel, but she holds behind her luring breast the combinations of water and fire, the elements that hold the powers of life and death. She can drown a man in an ocean of tears and she can resuscitate him with a flame of fire. She can reduce him to cinders with that same fire. These elements have an allegiance to her powers of emotions. A man has only to touch her and he becomes instantly inflamed with passion. Should he strike her, he has landed a death blow to his self. When she turns against him, he will be swept out to sea by the tide of her emotions. Women are indeed a living fire. After the rain came the thunder followed by the lightning.

"Look at them!" The Headmistress shouted as she pointed to the students who had followed her. "Look at what you have done to them. They are tired and under-nourished. You have turned them into slaves. Their parents are angry with you. At any day I expect them to come down on this school."

The Chief was not impressed by Mrs. Diop's demonstration. He remain stoic, keeping his restraint, but there was hot resentment in his face.

The Headmistress spoke on. "I am giving you fair warning, Chief. If you don't release the school's funds, you had better be prepared to lose everything. Your school will go. Your staff will go. Your students, your projects, your pigs."

That brought response. "My pigs!?" cried the Chief. He flew into a rage.

"Madam, did I not hear you mention my pigs? If you do not approve of how I am running this school, you may leave it."

He then turned to face the gathering crowd and shouted, "Listen to me!, all of you. It is I alone, Victor Ngomo Omubu, Chief of all Ijo Batanga, It is I who defied de parliament. I who own the lands of defeated Chiefs. I am de one who chose dis land to build a school. I cleared de forest. I cut de trees, and drove de mandrills into the forrest. It is I alone who knows de bite of de cobra, de sting of de scorpion, and de crush of de python and should any of you dare defy me, it is I who will have de last laugh, and that will be the laugh of de hyena over your corpses. Now leave me be, all of you."

The Chief walked up to the Headmistress. She stood dumbfounded. How could she possibly respond to this classical rhetoric of primitive insanity?

"And as for you, Madame " He spoke with an inane calmness, a penetrating stare. "Dis, my school, will be here long after you have returned to Scotland. Beware, Madame, Pundu here would love de taste of white flesh." Upon recognizing her name, Pundu's ear stood up.

The Headmistress wasted no further time. Pleading was useless but she had one more mission to accomplish, hand him the student's letter.

"Those, Chief, may very well be your famous last words" She said calmly and gave him the letter. He read its entirety:

"To Chief Victor Ngomo Mubu, Chief of Ijo Batanga, Proprietor of the Rogers Faircourt College. Mr. Omubu,

We the students of the Rodgers Faircourt College write this letter to you as a final warning. For too long have we suffered in silence. As you well know, we are not being properly fed. We have no clean water to drink or to wash with. We have no light to study by at night and our health is waning fast. Most of us cannot return to our homes. We have no money and we live too far. Is it not enough that our parents have paid our school fees? Those fees were to cover both our education and boarding.

Mr. Omubu, how long will we continue to suffer like this? If there are no changes in the next few days, we will not be held responsible for the consequences. Signed, Comrade Napoleon."

The Chief gazed up in questionable thought. "Comrade Napoleon? Who de hell is…?"

The student's letter demonstrated that the Headmistress had guided them through the *Animal Farm* textbook and after reading portions of Mao Tse-Tung's Little Red Book, they were comfortable with the use of the title "Comrade." Most of the countries of Africa were not so willing to plunge headlong into hard core Communist ideology but they were willing to experiment with the equally devastating doctrine of humanism, but not to the extent that it diametrically opposed fundamental Christianity. To the Christians in Africa, it was a "Christ centered universe." Humanism to them was a precocious vestibule to communist persuasions. The Chief, having been a Parliament veteran, was momentarily set back by their use of the word "comrade." It implied the majority against the minority. As far as the textbook was concerned, the Chief was oblivious to its existence.

CHAPTER 19

THE APPALLING CASE OF "MISTA VERTEBRA"

The singing beneath the window outside of my office was as clear as a parrot.

I took a quick peek out, not wanting to disturb it. To my surprise, the vocalist was none other than Mister Mukete, the Head Mistres's messenger. This was different from our first meeting, which was not a personal introduction, and to mention that we were not surrounded this time by a lot of students, I noticed that he had a very pronounced, highly curved vertebra which caused him to stand slightly bent. It was later that a student informed me that Mukete had been given the nickname of "Vertebra." Those students making mockery of him actually unabashedly called him "Mista Vertebra." It was a name that they should have been made to pay for, or at least reprimanded but those types of demeaning jest were never felt to be weighty enough to warrant discipline.

I felt that Mr. Mukete had enough disparaging tonnage to bear through life without having a name of scrimmage that was not given to him at his birth. The Science class students were responsible for the name calling out of sheer disrespect. They applied their chameleon skeleton collection to the physical likeness of this sad man.

I saw Mr. Mukete as a living portrait certainly after hearing him sing with such clarity, yet with a melancholy of purple. I thought of him rather as wounded bird. A bird that began his song while perched within the branches of a tree but then being struck in the wing by an arrow, he fell. Before the last drop of blood had flowed from him, he still found with in some means of the grace that was granted to him, to finish his melody while lying on the ground...and there, as he sang the final stanza of an African thanatopsis that is, the Song of Death. He was not aware that he was sharing a portion of that grace with me beneath my window.

To that I would simply say: Please be kind enough to allow a man to finish his song. For a song may be all that some men have, absolutely all that some men have.

How would I began to connect with Mukete? To begin with, I would call him "Mister." Today, I thought, I am going to make myself a new acquaintance.

I went out of my office and around the corner to the window with a cheerful "Good Morning, Mister Mukete!"

He seemed startled at first but rose to his feet, standing as much at attention as his deformity would allow. Previously he had been called Mister but always with a stigma attached. "Don't get up," I said, beckoning to him to sit back down. "You do speak some English, don't you?"

I knew that he did, but I had no idea how much English he spoke.

"Yis sah," He said with a smile. There was a glow in his eyes.

"Mister Mukete, tell me, just what are your duties here at the school?"

Mukete hesitated. "Well, you see sah, when I began here five years ago, I ask for the post of messenger."

I could detect disappointment as his bright smile arched "But isn't that what you are now a messenger?"

There simply had to be more to the story. There always is.

"Yes sah, but I was promised a post as a traveling messenger, sah, one who could travel from town to town by bicycle but now I am not permitted to go as far as the post office."

"How far away is the post office?" I asked.

"Eight miles, sah. It is a small house where mail is dropped off, sometimes every two weeks, sometimes three." "Well, who collects the school's mail now? Who runs long distance errands around here?"

Mukete slightly rubbed his head and answered, "De Chief does, sah." "Wait a minute you're telling me that Chief Omubu collects the school's mail?" "Yis sah, de Chief" He answered.

"Why does he do it and not you?"

"His driver takes him to de post, sah. De Chief opens de student's and de teacher's mail. On de day dat he took me with him, he sat in de motor and went through it all. He opened every last letter. Whenever he saw any monies or checks, he put dem in his pocket. He told me to keep my mouth shut or he would have me sacked. Since dat day, I just kept it quiet."

"So why now are you telling me this?" I asked.

Then came the answer that pierced my heart. "It's trust, sah, trust."

Trust is exactly what it would be between Mukete and me from that day forward. I had no idea that our trust would pay off because I can truthfully say that were it not for him, I would probably not be alive this day. I was charged by a fourteen foot Black Mamba and Mister Mukete distracted it and it went in another direction. I can still hear his voice as he yelled out to me, "Run, Mista Holiday! Run!"

The Chief's dirty little snooping had been whispered about during my arrival at the college but I had taken it lightly. Everyone was aware that the town mail was occasionally opened by security officials. They too were corrupt and could not be relied on, but no one dare to openly challenge any operation that was carried out in the name of National Security. It would be to the Chief's convenience should he decide to shift the blame on the officials should any suspicion should surfaces.

"But, Mister Mukete," I said. "Opening people's mail, that's a Federal Offense. He can't just go about opening people's mail."

Mukete gave me a puzzled look.

"Uh, excuse me sah . "What is a Fed de rawl offense?"

"What is a Federal Offense?" I answered. "That is when a crime has been committed against the Federal Government." At this answer we both burst out in laughter. I had forgotten which country I was in, and Mukete didn't gain any more from my parallel answer than when he had asked. "Oh, I no sabby dat one, sah. Dat one be na too strong fa my head,"

We both laughed about it again and the more so as I recalled that the African Constitutions are not based on the western Federal system.

"Mister Mukete, would you still care to have that Travelling Messenger's Post?" I asked.

He gave me no comment but sanctioned it with a nod. Years of wrinkled hardship seem to unravel from his face.

"Well, don't get your hopes too high, but I will try to speak to the Chief about it."

Mukete thanked me several times over as he started off gratefully clapping his hands in the usual African manner. I called him back. "You'll be given some different clothes and sandals even if you don't get the post."

He was now "Mister Mukete." I would make certain that the others about the campus would hear me address him so. I was not able to help him get promoted, but it was his God given right to have some recognized dignity. He was one of the myriads of a "never should have been history" and it was by an error of human design that the atrocities which did occur should have never happened, and were never meant to be recorded.

But, let us suppose for the sake of contemplative

speculation, that the label of "Mista Vertebra" that the students had given to him was not meant to be cruel, or even if it was intended to be mockery, such things have a way of returning to the cheerful giver the full measure of regret. For that very reason, it is obvious that there is no place for mockery in the universe of God. It is why God sent His only begotten Son into this universe to show the world how hideous it appears to be baptized by depraved men with the yellow spit of mockery, and afterwards He demanded that it be executed with all the other indictments on a cross.

Mr. Mukete went off to join in with the destiny of his Mother Africa as she wandered on her way through the dust-covered isles toward the sun set of history. He too would straddle the back of the inevitable as he had so often done before, as a warrior would stride his stallion and ride off into the unpredictable. Africa challenges men and women into miraculous survivors and molds them into what they have already proven to be.

CHAPTER 20

THE QUARREL – PART 1

It was now my turn at attempting to reason with the Chief. The Headmistress had tried, to no avail. It wasn't that I felt that I was any more skilled in trying to convince the Chief than she was, but it was necessary to let him know that there were others who were not intimidated by his furious responses. It was also important for him to know that every single person who challenge him did so not merely on their own, but was backed up by a consensus with equal potential.

But even there, there was a problem with the Headmistress and I approaching him. She and I were both foreigners and outsiders were known to infringe on authorities in Africa where they had no jurisdiction. The Chief would contend with us on those grounds. The problem was that not even one of his own countrymen would face him. They dare not attempt it, and the Chief was well aware of it. Should they ever initiate a confrontation with the Chief, he would retaliate with serious consequences. How would

I handle it? How would he respond to it? Had he calmed down now, after his clash with Mrs. Diop? In either case, it really wouldn't matter. The Chief would no doubt be pre-emptive to any one's attempt to reform him or to tell him how he should run his establishment. All the same, he had to be faced.

Early the following morning, after a sleepless night, I took a stroll up to Lake Brumbi to think things over. My intentions were to return to the college in the afternoon, about the time when Chief Omubu would arrive to attend to his pigs. To him, this was a religious appointment that he had to keep The pouring out libations of wine, singing the sacred "Fumyta Hymn of the Pigs," taking a deep breath of their putrid stench and seeing to it that they were well fed with the student's maize.

The lake was a volcanic extension of a chain of under-ground corridors that frequently belched out lava from time to time. It was just five years ago that a subterranean erup-tion spilled molten lava out into the lake bottom. The lake became an instant caldron that was so seething that poison gas released and killed many of the villagers in the area. Of course nothing in Africa goes to waste but human lives, and those who escaped the heat took advantage of the bonanza of fish that covered the surface of the lake.

The awesome beauty of the lake was magnetic, and so serene that it was hard to imagine how anyone could have had such a tragic ending there. Just to see it from the top of the hill that I was on was captivating. The panoramic view of the emerald forest that covered the hills surrounding the lake, the fog and the mist that rested in the valleys which were summon by the sun to rise again and amble its vapors causing the streams below to flow in artisan ripples. There was fresh dew on everything and especially visible were the diamond kisses that it left on not a single neglected blade of thankful grass. Chimpanzees' echoes were heard from hill to hill when they screamed.

The natives that now surrounded the lake continue to take their chances as they lived with its uncertainties. They took their folk lore quite seriously, believing that there were spirits, treacherous spirits, living at the bottom of the lake. These were said to have taken women as captives from time to time and perform their nocturnal rites on innocent bodies. They believe that somewhere down there beneath the black and green maelstrom, under the death chants of juju priests who have been long dead, the curly haired, red eyed, weeping virgin's black bodies were offered as they writhed in futility just before their trickling blood would quench the thirst of the angry gods.

The African night possess a power of its own and is believed to summon her nocturnal children who claim that the night spirits empowers Runners to perform acts that are prohibited in the light of the day. They are feared because they are believed to kidnap and sacrifice infants, decapitate adults and sell their skulls to black markets that make a profit trafficking them off to certain Islamic countries.

As little as I realized it, human skulls are in great demand in various parts of the world, and if it so happens that there is a shortage in the underworld market, there are those who will murder to get their hands on one. I was informed that for some reason, fresh skulls are preferred above old ones.

Why? It may be the fact that witchcraft is global.

These Night Runners are believed to have perfect vision in the dark, but are unable to see no more than a few blurry feet during the day. Since their deeds were evil, I could not allow the dark to overtake me since I was quite a distance from my home. There I stood, holding two papers in my hands. They were exactly the same in length and width. The ink which they were written was nothing more than what it was, "ink" I had to weigh the difference between the importance of the letters.

The first letter that I received was written by a student, a girl who wrote it during her free composition class. The students were allowed to express themselves in any way that they felt The girl wrote about her mother, who was very ill back in her village. She lived several hundred miles away. She also spoke of her father who wasn't doing much better physically as he had to work very hard on their small patch of land to survive without any support.

More importantly, I was touched by an excerpt she wrote, changing her subject and began to describe how she regretted signing up with the Roger's Faircourt College.

"My biggest mistake," she began, "was being born into this world. I have seen so many people suffer, especially nowadays. Life is difficult. You have to be educated to live a better life. I remember that the mistake I made was to come here to this terrible school, eating beans all the time. If only

I knew before what I know now, I never would have applied to enter this horrible place. All I can see here are trees, bushes which I am forced to clear away and this awful mud during the rainy season. When you try to walk, it sticks to your shoes and the more you walk, the more it accumulates. It just tires you out. By the time you reach your class and scrape it off, you are too tired to study or do anything else.

Here we work like animals to support the animals especially the pigs. We are forced to do things that our parents do not know about. I only pray to God every day to get me out of this place. All I ever hear from the Chief is pigs, pigs. I believe that he carries their spirit in his bosom."

That letter, of course was far weightier than the other one. The other letter was disgusting. The Chief had instructed the Headmistress to inform me of a change of my duties. Staggeringly enough, and without the least bit of compunction or regard for my wife whom he knew was ill, and for me who had not received a salary, he sent me the second letter.

"Mr. Holiday; I have been instructed by the Chief to inform you of your change of duties. There is an urgent need for your assistance in the Bursar's Office. Due to a death in his family, he will not be returning for quite some time. You will be working in that capacity for several days. When you have completed your assignment there, you will resume your overall assignments as well as teaching where needed. For now, I have assigned Mr. S. Etah to teach in your place. He will afterwards assist you with the syllabus when you are ready.

Thank you kindly,

S. Diop, Headmistress."

As I read the letter, I could see Mrs. Diop bursting her sides with laughter, not because she was happy to see me miserable but perhaps she was imagining my angry response. If that was what she was thinking, she was entitled to a good laugh, because I had gone beyond anger. I was sizzling.

CHAPTER 21

THE QUARREL – PART II

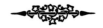

Mrs. Diop was right and so was Tandangu and all the others. The Roger's Faircourt was not merely a dying school, it was on the fringes of a disastrous ending.

Today, I would face the Chief. I recalled that when I first arrived at the school, I deliberately refused to accept the awful rumors I had heard about him no matter how somber they sounded. I had to see it for myself.

Since I had fantasized to extremes about Africa and about how communal and traditional she was. It was difficult for me to come to a truce with reality. My fantasizing had nearly become fanatic to the point that I had deceived myself into believing that it had become a part of me and that to destroy that image would have been to destroy a part of myself.

No power on earth could have made me believe that what I was seeing for my first few years in Africa could actually happen in Africa. When I witnessed my first public execution of six men tied to poles in front of sand bags. It had a horrendous effect on me.

When I saw a man, just skin and bones lying in the streets of Africa, gasping his last breath, and taxies were driving round him trying to avoid running over him, while over on the side walk there stood men smoking cigarettes, refusing to pick him up, I just couldn't believe it. I took a sheet from my motel and rushed to cover his nakedness I was forbidden to do so. The man laid in the streets all night until finally, the next day, before sun rise, he died and the angels carried him home. Now that glass of illusion that I carried in my bosom about Africa had been shattered and behind its jagged edges lay the naked realities.

There were evil things happening around me that I was refusing to see or believe. The Chief was part of that evil Africa, not the mother country that I had hoped. In the eyes of the Chief's country men, he stood an insensitive unabashed glutton, who was enmeshed into a deeply rooted occult that only he and his swine could have entry into, while his tribesmen who would have been loyal to him, were pushed away by his indifference about their plight.

The Chief could find no other basis for his actions other than on his very own inane, self-styled, mercurial whims. It is always justifiable when a man reaches that level of maturity when he can thrust aside his unrealistic dreams and confront the evils that his dreams had glossed over. Not every evil can be done away with by the use of carnal weapons. It takes moral courage to do the will of God and God Himself will be the weapon. That is called "meekness accompanied by a supernatural Companion."

Chief Omubu was definitely not a person who could be approached with a grievance in an amicable way. As Papa Bouambo had said, he was a wounded lion on the rampage. Sacked from the Parliament, hurtfully embarrassed, with an eye for vengeance against any one that walked on two legs, a cannibal who had a craving for destruction and would devour everyone within his reach until, finally, there would be nothing left to consume but his self. Afterwards, he would sit about, gazing upon his own splintered bones, for which he would have no further use than for a toothpick.

At best, had the opportunity availed, he would have become another Baby Doc, at his worst, an Idi Amin. As fate would have it, the good people of Ijo Batanga were given Chief Omubu, a man who loved only to wine and dine with his swine until they blushed with oinks and squeals.

Until now, the Chief had been fond of me, but I was aware that his fondness was strictly conditional. It was based on my remaining nothing more than a harmless spectator, an indifferent side liner, a novice in Africa. Perhaps he had taken me for someone who was oblivious to the African ways of life, or maybe I would be easy enough for him to use, as he would his own walking stick. For quite some time, I had kept silent about the Chief's bizarre ways and he liked it that way.

What the chief did not know, was that one day, I would unmask myself, cast aside my garment of silence and reveal to him a side of me that could not tolerate seeing others suffer. I had been given more than my share of it. Until now, without even trying to make a point of it, I could actually live in Africa among my brothers under the most strenuous circumstances. Never once did I glance back over my shoulder to the black men in America who are enjoying their post- slavery freedom and cry, "Thank God for slavery." I did not come to Africa to prove that I could suffer any more than I left America because I was receiving first class citizen status. I merely came to Africa to live and to learn.

That is exactly what I did. I lived and I learned. I lived with hungry days and nights and I learned to love away the bitterness that had often raged in my heart. I learned to walk from eight to ten miles on an empty stomach to buy food and I learn to share all that I had with stranded families who sat all night at my door waiting for me to feed them. I learn what it was to lie on a bed burning with malaria fever while I waited my turn to pass through death's door. I learn how to turn my face to the wall and cry with what little strength was left for God to release me, dispatch me to His home above or bring me back to life and restore me to His service. I learn to trust in Him who gave breath to the flies that surrounded me and a heartbeat to the mosquitoes that harpooned me to my death bed.

In His great mercy and by His life giving breath, He stood me back up on my feet again. When I smelled the stench of those three hundred black women who had been gunned down, I learn to love every man that walks on this God owned earth but I hated the evil that cried out that their deaths were justified because their skin was not the color of the fingers that pulled those triggers.

I went directly toward the piggery. Passing by the

school's galley, I noticed the cooks sitting idly, not having anything to cook. The beans had run out. One of them shouted, "I go fa strike, sah, My pikin get no chop fa belly. I got woman. She don get belly fa pikin. Chief don't pay me. I no work."

I understood what he meant. His children were not eating. He had a wife who was pregnant. He was now on a strike because the Chief refused to pay him for his services. Some of the workers had already begun to steal what they needed for their families. They ran into the forest with yams, chickens, rabbits, and as much maize as they could hold.

I saw the Chief from a distance. He was in his favorite spot, leaning as usual on the top of the worn fence, which could have collapsed at any time from his weight. He stared calmly at his pigs. It was a sinister calm one would wonder if whether or not he was aware of the prevailing uneasiness that was closing in on him. He certainly put up an impressive pretension of a blatant indifference regarding it. Obviously he would not surrender passionately without a fight. He was like the cobra that he claimed to have power over. He would only strike when you came within striking distance. On the other hand, he appeared to be like the proverbial frog that was so confident that even when it had been placed into a pot of cool water and laid on a red hot stove, it could not escape when it began to boil.

I would seize those seconds that lay between him and me to modify Lincoln's speech. "You can starve some of the people some of the time, but you can't starve all of the people all of the time."

Severe hunger and thirst will unite the most diametri-cally opposed people anywhere on the planet. Whether they be predator or prey, they will come together for the com-mon cause. One of the reasons there is so much prejudice in America is because there is an overabundance of food sources. But let that supply dwindle to a mere morsel and blacks and whites and all of "God's chillin" will unite in a deer hunt and divide the kill. They will come together in fellowship, sing and dance, and forget all of their differences until their hunger is quelled and their thirst quenched. After that, its "Back to the hills!"

"Chief," I called as I walked up to him. He looked at me but kept silent. He could tell by the tone of my voice that my truce of silence was over.

"You have got to pay your people their salaries, or at least release your farm produce over to them."

The Chief slowly straightened up from his position and with the most uncanny look in his eyes, he spoke. "Mista Holiday, Did I hire you to probe into my personal affairs?"

"This, Chief, is no longer a matter of personal affairs. It is every body's business. You gave me a responsible as-signment as Bursar, making me accountable for every one's salaries. I cannot stand idly by and watch them suffer. There is nothing but a rubber band in the safe. When did it be-come African to starve people?"

That was a direct insult to the Chief. I knew it and I intended for it to be.

"African!" he shouted. "What do you know about de

African? You know noting about de African. You came from a family of slaves."

"Yes," I snapped. "You're right. I came from a family of slaves that were your family's blood relatives from right out of your own blood line. Your family were the people who betrayed and sold their own sons and daughters off into slavery and neither you nor your people are another franc richer for it. In fact, it has made you poorer and that very evil, Chief, can be easily traced back to your doorstep, seeing as how you have betrayed these laborers and students. By the way, Chief, it was one of your slave relatives who said that No man's happiness cannot be purchased by another man's misery."

By this time the Chief was furious. I am not so sure that he heard every word that I said, but he did get some of it.

"Watch your mouth, my friend! Do you know who you are talking to? Do you dink because I walk about wearing my native attire and bare footed dat I am not an educated man? Dat I am a primitive savage? I know all about your twisted history books."

CHAPTER 22

THE INCITER

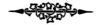

It had been mentioned that the students compared the *Animal Farm* story to those ongoing events occurring on their campus. Now another situation has surfaced where Chief Omubu's name had been coined. It was by a Form Four student, Nwele M'bongo, a popular figure at the school. He too, was the son of a Chief, a young, unrecognized prince. His father lived over five hundred miles away and had no jurisdiction in the Batanga district.

It was during the evening when the students were in their classes quietly preparing for the following days lessons. "That is who he is!" shouted Nwele." That is exactly who he is! "

The other students who willingly welcomed the slightest interruptions, all joined in: "That is who he is?" they chorused.

"Quiet, you guys!" warned the Form Monitor who was another student whose status was selected on his behavior merit. "Another outburst like that and you'll leave me no choice but to write down your names and turn them in tomorrow for punishment."

"Can we be punished any more than what we are?" Nwele retorted. "Why is it that you tell me to stop making noise when I have made a discovery?" Nwele, conjuring a consensus, stood on the top of his chair and spoke out again. "Answer me!" he added. "Can we undergo any worse punishment than what we are now receiving?"

He then pointed to the Form Monitor and faced the class. "He is no different than we are and if he is willing to admit it, he too is suffering just as much as we are."

Nwele now had the student's undivided attention. Other students, hearing the commotion, abandoned their classrooms and ran to listen in as their Monitors followed after them shouting "punishment." Nwele spoke on. "Look at me! Look at yourselves! Do not your stomachs pain as I speak? What worse than death can overtake us?

"You all came to this college happy and healthy. But look at you now you are nothing more than just a bunch of sticks, walking sticks, ready to make the Chief's bonfire brighter. If my father should see me now, he would cry, "Who is this that is coming into my hut? I sent my son away to school but a stick has returned." "How anyone could rightfully call this place a college, or even a school?" Nwele held up the *Animal Farm* text book. "This is who he is!" he shouted.

"Tell us," asked a student from the back of the class. "What are you talking about? Who is who?"

"The Chief, you idiot I'm speaking about Chief Omubu.

He is exactly like the Mister Jones in this textbook. He is eating fufu, eggs, yams, fish, and fowl. His stomach speaks for him. We eat nothing but beans that weevils have bored holes in our stale bread."

The Form Monitor, seeing that he was in the minority, moved closer to listen. Everyone had rallied around Nwele. As his crowd became larger, the consensus grew. It was as though Nwele had received an epiphany. He preached on and on as if he was destined to incite rebellion. Within minutes he had become a natural, a conflagrant Decembrist, self-knighted, and born out of the needs of sympathy for his fellow man. He had become newly acquainted with his self. What would he become, a hero or a tyrant?

In either case he was born out of oppression. He had the ability to fire others up, to galvanize those hungry, timid students into a mob of foaming blood lust. He stirred their passions and replaced their hunger with the desperate desire to get revenge.

Setting a banquet before them now would have made little difference. They would have considered it as part of the spoil, nothing more. In the absence of the teachers that night, the school belonged to Nwele. While the rest of the school rested and the Chief snored with visions of pigs dancing in his head, a small revolution was being born. The man who strikes the match determines where the fire will start but he has no control of how far it will spread, the amount of damage it will cause, or when it will burn out.

"The Chief lives in a comfortable house filled with luxury," he shouted." But we have no electricity and no clean water. He has a generator, but we must burn candles to study by. We are forced every day to carry buckets from the stream. We are forced to risk our lives from crocodiles and angry hippos. We carry sand on our heads in order that he can build bigger rooms for his pigs. Our parents are paying dear for our fees but all we are getting are filthy latrines that are on the verge of an epidemic."

Nwele raised his arms high above his head to prove his point. He clenched his fist as he cried, "Death to Mister Jones and his men!"

I heard about this excitement long after it was over. It was scary when I thought about it. It sent chills down my spine, especially when I heard the phrase "to his men."

Was Nwele a sizzling anarchist just waiting to be flipped over on his other side onto the hotplate of life and to be fried until he was well done? Or would he one day become a credit to Africa?

Was he simply unaware that he had become an apprentice to his powerful enemy, Chief Omubu? Would he simply emulate the very man whose ways caused him so much misery, as so many men often do? Would he become a credit to Africa? Would that very class room become a museum some day after he had risen to fame honoring him as a legend and would that very chair on which he had given his speech be gilded with gold in tribute to him? Or would he burst like a bubble and become a magnet for maggots, attracting the scum of the earth? Perhaps his speech was a mere perforated, piffled platitude, a closed book about a tiny school in the middle of a forgotten forest in Africa.

In some places stars are born and they die. In other places stars die and then they are reborn to breathe the praise worthy of eternal martyrs. In other places, men become delusional stars who die in infamy and are glorified by their deceived admirers. In any case, at some time or another, they all die.

From that night and for the next few days, it was as though nothing had occurred. But after Nwele had stepped down from off of his classroom chair nothing again at that school would ever be the same. It was difficult to believe how quiet five hundred students could be. Not a single leak about Nwele's speech was mentioned. No further complaints were heard. Every student was well behaved. There was not the slightest hint of consternation. They ate their beans with glad pretense and requested loudly for more beans when their platters were empty. It was without a doubt that someone was in charge. An abnormal peacefulness had become so conspicuous that the Discipline Master jokingly walked out to the front of the campus to read the Faircourt college sign, to be sure that he was still at the same college.

CHAPTER 23

THE TRUTH ABOUT LOVE

It was in Africa where I discovered that falling in love with the God of all creation was an indescribable reality, a tenacious and a meta-chromatic quest that is so timeless that it sweetens time itself. It reduces space to the dimensions of a living room and then gives to it a destiny that once again expands its arms to embrace the stars. That is what love causes. It is an indescribable mixture of nonsensical descriptions that stir dormant emotions that when they are awaken, fly far beyond the boundaries of taste and time and silence the rhetoric of heart and tongue and leave us in a state of glorified wordlessness.

For me, to love God more than life itself, grew out of my increasingly tortured awareness that I was by far the unworthy that caused the unworthy to blush.

However, God does bring his love to the unlovely and to the unlovable. I exhausted those two descriptions. I was a filthy rag hung out to dry by the imps of hell, to be used again to absorb the scum of the earth.

Even the unlovely and the unlovable need to be loved. It is not a question as to whether they deserve it or not. That question has already been settled. It is the need that they have that still remains. It is a need that only God can fill. He placed a love in my care.

She was one of Africa's most charming daughters of competitive beauty: the chocolate skin, her ultricious hair that allures a man to bury his face into it and take a deep breath from the surface of her golden bowl, pressing so close to her roots that he can catch the aroma of her ravishing thoughts, and a smile that revealed the whitest teeth that only the Creator could have placed those alluring pair of eyes, which held me captive. Such a purity of spirit of untarnished transparency. Her name was Carol.

I had ventured far into the forest, following one of Papa Boambu's suggestions.

"Go into the forest" he would say. "Perhaps your answer is out there waiting."

My answer was there. I was searching for her without knowing it. There she was, standing in the palm of God's hand beneath a splattering waterfall.

If a man says that he has never loved or that he has never been loved, then he has either lied about it or he has never allowed love to conquer his heart. A man must always be reaching out for that part of himself that is missing, that refined element, that exquisite beauty that exist in the artistic form of the creation's replica of the Mother of all living (Eve).

A man is incomplete without that natural nurse who

can heal him with only three words. He needs her to fill his void, to gaze at her flesh transformed into flowers of music while pondering over the phenomenal question, "What was God thinking when He made her?"

Men's hearts are made for love. It is the only thing that a man has never conquered. Men have conquered cities, nations, empires and even a tiny portion of outer space, but no man has ever accomplished a quest, nor will he ever over power love. Men are captured and enslaved by love. Love has never been conquered by man. Even after he has been vanquished by love, contrary to his thinking, a man is at his weakest when he is in the act of love's conjugal union. The heart was never created to hate. It was made only to be captured by love.

Whenever hate invades the heart, it comes in as a destructive alien. Its sole purpose is to destroy the heart in order that it may never love again. The only way to overcome hate's design is to open the flood gate of the heart and be overcome by the conquering river of Love.

After introducing ourselves, Carol and I began a discussion of the whereabouts of the location of the Garden of Eden.

"I suppose that it might have been located somewhere within the region of ancient Mesopotamia." I said. I am sure that God has hidden it from the eyes of mankind. If he hadn't, then it is without a doubt that some religious group would claim it for its own or you would have to pay to take a tour of it. Of course, the Tree of Life would be guarded by soldiers. That was why God placed cherubim at its entrance, to keep the Way open to the human race in order that they will re enter someday by the awesome blood price paid by the Son of God.

Carol was a woman of few words. She just smiled in agreement at my words. I decided to apply the topic to her and me. "As far as I am concern," I added, "This is the Garden of Eden and you and I are Adam and Eve."

Carol immediately realized what I was getting at and she laughed uncontrollably. From that day, hardly a week went by that we did not meet some where. We often met at the top of the crater lake or in the forest near the waterfall. Word had gotten out at the school that we had become far more than mere acquaintances.

Of course, it was all right with me. It is a bit odd in Africa for a man not to have a companion. I once saw a man there who was so deformed that he actually crawled on his all fours to get around. His hands and his knees were callused with thick layers of skin but his tribe's men saw to it that he was given a wife to look after him. She also bare him children. They were all born without any physical defect. They respected their father to the highest and served him well.

I had mentioned previously about how Africans will not hesitate to express their approval or disapproval about your involvement with the company that you keep. They felt it their duty to act as a guard on my behalf.

Years ago there was a similar custom in America among black people. If a young woman or man wish to court one another, their parents would express great concern as to whether or not a suitor's parents, as well were church members, who was their pastor, were the family decent people, et cetera? The parents also presided over the courtship. No kissing or cussing was allowed and the man had to show all due respect to the parents of the girl. Engagements were as big a celebration as was the marriage. If a girl became pregnant during the courtship, marriage was inevitable.

How times have changed! These days a man will live with a woman for fifteen years or more, have several children together, and never once think enough of her to ask her hand in marriage. They will claim each other as fiancés. Certain parents will allow the youngsters to cohabit within their homes, just to keep their daughters from rebelling. They have forgotten or have never known that only the slaves were not allowed to get married. Many of our fore fathers died with broken hearts after they had begged for years to be allowed to be married but were refused permission to do so. Today, so many African Americans seem to take pleasure in living under slave laws.

Carol and I were given a customary wedding. A small dowry of two goats and a barrel of mealy meal were given and well-wishers from surrounding villages brought donations of chickens, furniture and baskets, most of which were handed to her parents. We received their blessings and moved into our house within the school compound.

For a while we managed our affairs without any difficulty. Although our food supply was meager, we were able to eat enough. Many of our neighbors joined in with us at meals. We men shared our meals together from the same bowl, as did the women. It took a while for me to get used to, it but it was either that, go hungry, or risk friendships. My African wife was now pregnant.

Since I couldn't afford to lose anything, I adopted the old saying, with small modification. "When in Africa, do as the Africans do."

It was later that things began to shatter again when the Chief decided to once again, withhold our salaries, and at the worst possible time. Carol was now in her sixth month of pregnancy and she wasn't doing well at all. She lacked the vitamins that she needed and there were no doctors in the area. There was a distance of ten miles between the college and the make shift clinic. There were no doctors there. They made only annual appearances to give inoculations to newborns. The government hospital was well over a hundred and fifty miles away. Everything was scarce medicine, food, electricity and all water had to be boiled. Carol grew up in this type of environment but it is not one that anybody could adequately adjust to. Why does a man have to be admonished when the drastic need for his services are ubiquitously evident about him?

CHAPTER 24

SILHOUETTE

The intensified scream in the forest was once again the bush baby's announcement that darkness was approaching, signaling his nocturnal companions. Like a clock, though quite a small creature, his deafening cry made him the "Big Ben" of the forest.

The night blooming jasmine released their melodious flow of fragrance, giving a welcome relief from the overwhelming odor of the pigs. Night scenes were played out in their timeless harmony of the nocturnal myriads. Giant fruit bats by the thousands began darkening the skies, hurriedly shutting out what was left of the faintest amber of sun set.

Classes were over and the students were so worn out from their farm work and their studies that they dragged themselves to their dormitories and crashed out on their bunks. There were times when the girls could be heard singing the sweetest songs, but tonight even they were just too tired.

No sooner had I opened my door, than I heard a faint groaning coming from our bedroom. It was Carol. She was doubled over in pain.

"What is it?" I asked.

"I don't know, I don't know," she groaned. "It feels like the baby is coming,"

Before going on with this story, I want to mention again that my wife, Carol, is a beautiful woman. She is an adorable woman in fact, she is amazing. The very sight of her often puts me to shame when I am reminded of my naughty thoughts. She still holds that gift of overwhelming purity within her bosom that many women possess, and when I see her, it is then that I realize that I am so unworthy of her touch.

So many times, due to the hardships of the college, I had tried my best to convince her to return to her parents until after the baby was born, but she insisted on remaining there with me.

"I cannot leave you here alone," she exclaimed, as she held onto her paining tummy with one hand, gently stroking my face with the other. "It is not our custom for a wife to leave her husband for any reason. If we must die, it must be together."

Try writing that in the marriage vows of the western world, I thought. *But for the sake of life, it should be done.*

I raced out of the house onto MBonge Road. What often seems like an eternity in Africa has strange ways of working out. After a short time, the lights of a Land Rover were seen approaching. I stood in the road waving it down.

Most Africans will stop. The inconveniences of Africa have mandated it so. The driver stopped.

"What tiz it my Broda?" he asked.

"My wife, she's having a baby. Could you take us to the clinic? Please."

"Yes, yes," he repeated. The driver rushed in to the house with me and helped me carry Carol out.

The ride to the Clinic was a rough dirt road all the way. A few goliath rats and several dik diks were seen sprinting across in front of us. The ride itself was rugged enough to cause a miscarriage.

Finally we arrived at the clinic. To our dismay, the gate was locked and the watchman was sound asleep. That is typical in Africa. He had nothing to watch for. However, due to recent guerrilla fighting in that area, who would burst in and raid the clinic and take any medicines? Most gates were secured.

"Open please!" I yelled.

The watchman opened his eyes and slowly dragged himself over to the gate holding his night stick under his arm. "Say na whiti?" he asked in pidgin English.

The driver became so disgusted that he began to curse in his own language, but I did manage to hear him squeeze out, "silly goose!" Finally, in plain English, "Open de dam gate we are having a baby,"

In contrast to the watchman, the one midwife on duty worked with dedication. She needed me to assist her. I was about to cave in, but I couldn't let her know it. The sight of so much blood nauseated me. I became dizzy and about to pass out but I kept lying to myself, saying, "Men don't faint! Men just don't faint!"

The Midwife looked at me. She knew something was wrong.

"Are you all right, sah?" she asked.

"As can be expected, Madame" I nervously answered.

The baby came out. It was so tiny, smaller than normal. The Midwife passed the child to me. It was a boy covered with blood, the navel cord still attached. I teared up.

Carol would be in pain, but the midwife was able to give her something for it. The Midwife quickly dabbed the sweat from her forehead, severed the navel cord and gently cleaned the baby. She handed the child to me. "You have a son." She said. "What will you name him?"

I gazed at him." What a beautiful boy," I exclaimed. "Silhouette," I answered. His name is Silhouette.

I was about to speak again when she softly interrupted. "But, sah, I am afraid there is something which you must know." Her countenance became grave. "The child is just too small, sah. It is quite doubtful that he will live. He might live for a day or for just a few hours, but beyond that, we cannot say."

"But there are no incubators here?"

"No, sah," she said sadly, shaking her head slowly and looking me straight in the eyes. "I am very sorry, sah, but we have nothing like that here."

As she spoke, I felt as though the earth had given away beneath me. "You mean to say, nurse, that in the whole of this place, there are no incubators?"

"Yes," she replied. "Not one single incubator. We are always losing our babies here for that very same reason. You must know that our facilities here are very limited. No incubators, no oxygen, no way to prepare food for our patients. Most people are brought here to quarantine a disease to keep it contained and to keep it from spreading. Even some of our medicines, which we have, are expired."

"But what about the nearest hospital?" I asked. "Can you borrow an incubator from them?"

The Midwife looked at me and while expressing with open hands she said, "Sah, to be truthful, the nearest hospital is so far from here that by the time it would take us to ask for permission from our Ministry, sign several forms after filling them out, find transportation and bribe the junior and the senior officers within the Ministry, it would take us many days to get it here. Besides, the Administrators of the nearest hospital that I have in mind are all whites. They are a growing community and they feel that they will need them for their own people." The midwife continued. "There is simply nothing that we can do about it, sah. You must also know that you're wife's condition is critical. She has lost a lot of blood and weight. What she needs is a lot of nourishment."

The midwife was right. Having much experience within her profession, she showed a tremendous amount of dedication. She knew exactly what brought it all on. "Apparently" she said when Mrs. Carol was carrying the baby, she wasn't getting enough to eat."

That Chief! I couldn't help but think. "Is it possible that

my wife could get a blood transfusion?"

"It would be possible only if our refrigerator was working, sah. It broke down some months ago. All of the blood that we had went bad. In fact, receiving somebody else's blood in this part of Africa…" she hesitated. "I would be very careful about it, sah."

"Please, may I see my wife and baby?"

"Yes, go right in."

Carol was lying half asleep in a bed next to the baby. I walked over to the woven straw basket where the child was sleeping and lifted the blue mosquito net lay across its top. Silhouette was so tiny that I could have placed him in a tea cup. Such a handsome little boy not much hair, and his skin was almost transparent, showing his tiny veins. The midwife was right. He was entirely too small but I just couldn't give up. Not as long as there was life.

He may be small I thought, but I wanted to convince myself that he looked strong enough. It was all wishful thinking.

Africa's infant mortality rate is perhaps the highest in the world. Infant souls are flying out of Africa one in every four before their first year is completed. They too will unite with the holy family of heaven alongside the fifty million aborted infants of America and its population of deceased little ones and others the world over, and stand beside the holy angels and with their glorious shrills of empyreal ecstasy they will join in the Hallelujah anthem of the King of Kings and give Him thanks for rescuing them from out of this filthy world.

I reached into the basket and placed his tiny finger on mine. I whispered, "Please don't leave me, son. Let's explore Africa together. Let's began our own little *Roots* program."

Silhouette's tiny face gave me a smile. The old folks used to say that when a baby smiles, he sees the angels. Suddenly his smile went away. A slight frown took its place as he continued his rapid breathing. It seemed as though he was fighting to stay on in the best way that he could.

Carol awoke. I explained all to her that the midwife had said. She burst into tears. A voice called out "Mista Holiday. Come, please."

It was the midwife beckoning for me from the veranda. She was holding a blood stained bundle wrapped in some newspaper and put into a plastic bag.

"What is it?" I asked, assuming that perhaps it was some of Carol's clothes.

"It is your baby's navel cord and placenta sah" She answered.

"But why give it to me? What am I supposed to do with it? Could you kindly dispose of it for me?"

The midwife gravely, but gently insisted. There are some discussions that Africans will avoid if they possibly can. "You should either burn it or bury it," she said. "Some people here keep their naval cords for safety."

"Safety? Safety from what?"

If you are too insistent, you will often get the answer that you are not ready for.

"Oh no, sah," She responded with a serious face. "We don't usually dispose of such things as this. We leave it up to the parents to do with it what they wish. We don't want to be blamed if anything should happen."

"If anything should happen? What could possibly happen to a naval cord? And what could happen any worse than having a dying child, other than its death? I've had enough problems for one day. Just let your people do away with it."

The Midwife looked at me with a slight smile. She then gave a big sigh and said, "Sah, forgive me. I should have explained it to you before. You see, our people are very superstitious and many of them are very wicked. They can work evil with the smallest things a finger nail, and a toe nail, the hair left in your comb or even your very feces that is, if they hate you enough. Especially in matters of witchcraft. They would pay a lot of money just to get their hands on this very navel cord. They even have people working at hospitals who keep an eye out for careless people who walk away and leave these things, an employee or anybody. You never know who's working for them. They would watch where you buried your child's navel cord, then go right behind you and dig it up again, dry it out, grind it to powder, and use it against you or someone in your family."

I was speechless.

Then she added, "You don't know Africans like I do. That is the very reason that some of our Presidents and Chiefs have assigned a 'Royal Keeper of the navel cord' to protect it. That is an ancient practice that goes all the way back to only God knows when. If possible, that assignment is given to their grandmothers."

She was right again. I didn't know Africans like she knew

them. But neither did I know Americans and Europeans like I thought I knew them. All continents are inundated with superstition, the glorification of science, devil worship, secret societies that claim that they have received some higher knowledge that is exclusive to themselves, rituals of infant sacrifices, including those on the altars of surgical tables, altered states of consciences, cannibalism, and banks that are bulging from their revenues. That is why the Holy Bible calls money "filthy lucre," not only because it passes from hand to hand, but because of the spiritual filth that it is transacted by.

Only Heaven knows what is happening with in the Kingdom of Heaven. As someone said, Satan is a legitimate card carrying member of the Kingdom of Heaven. The exclusives that are in the right standing are within the Kingdom of God. Of course, if a man is not in the right standing then it stands to reason that he is not standing right. Being top heavy with delusional pride and arrogance can cause any one to fall over. Again, as I said, Pride comes before a fall and an arrogant spirit before one's destruction. It is a part of the fabric of the universe. Tear apart that cosmic needle work, and you tear a breach in your short future. The finite woven thoughts of man are opposed to the infinite needlework of God. God can either lay a man across His knees and patch his pants while he is wearing them or place him across His knees and tan his hide. The first move is up to the man.

The midwife handed me the package and proceeded down the hall. She paused and came back. "What is the meaning of the name Silhouette, sah?"

"It refers to the outline of something," I answered. "I see him as the outline of all that is pure. And I had hoped that someday, he would have filled that outline with all that is honest, sincere and righteous in the sight of God."

CHAPTER 25

THE BURIAL

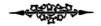

Sadly, it happened. Little Silhouette passed away on the very night of his birth. "A tiny spirit with thought swift wings flew from his little black house, transcended constellations, nebulae, and a billion one-way twilight zones to repose in the sun whirling arms of God."

I was carrying the body of my son and the package from his birth as I started back on the ten-mile walk. *Surely the hyenas will pick up the scent*, I thought as I began my journey. Most of them are intimidated by the presence of humans but I was more concerned about the leopards. They were in the area.

Mr. Ekoko and Mr. Namme, another teacher, had heard about our misfortune and started walking on the MBonge road to meet me. We made contact. Ekoko and Namme were a welcome sight and a relief to those uncertainties. Both men rushed to my side.

"We are terribly sorry indeed sah."

"We are truly without words." were their only comments.

We walked along togather in silence for some time. Finally they said, "Uh, if you don't mind, sah, we will began digging the grave as soon as we reach the compound."

"Please, if you will." I answered.

"We don't want the students to know about this if you don't mind, sah," Ekoko advised.

"It would take something like this to start them on a rampage. It would only fuel the fire that they have against the Chief."

"But we will need a shovel," suggested Namme. "We will be near the Chief's house. I'm sure he wouldn't mind us borrowing his shovel. Besides, we think that he should know about your sorrow."

"By him being the Chief, he should be the first to know," suggested the other.

At the time I didn't think it was a good idea but in Africa, customs must be allowed to run their course.

Ekoko spoke up. "We haven't the time nor the means to make a coffin, sah, and it wouldn't be good to leave the body unburied for long. We can bury the child somewhere near the college campus. These are matters which should be disposed of as soon as possible, at least before tomorrow's sunrise. In this part of Africa, we never leave bodies above ground for long."

"Allow me to carry the baby sah," Ekoko ask.

"Thank you, Mr. Ekoko." I replied. "It's very kind of you, but if you don't mind, I'd rather carry him."

I held on to Silhouette for as long as I could. keeping a firm grip against my chest as though I still had to protect him. Fatherly and motherly instincts can be very tenacious, even after the death of a child, no matter how long or brief the child may live. Instead of fading away, the instincts grow stronger, for love itself is stronger than death.

We walked about eight miles before we reached the Chief's house. I could feel the damp night dew as it settled like a cold sheet across my hands and face.

Insects and frogs chanted in concert like a mourning choir. Mosquitoes surrounded us like an aura, drawn by our body heat and perspiration. They became frantic, stinging where they could, reminding us that they were the agents of death and that there was no pity that they could offer for the mourning or for the dead.

We finally arrived at the Chief's house. Ekoko knocked lightly. Fortunately for us there were no dogs around to threaten us. They were no doubt battling it out with the hyenas. There was no answer and he knocked again. Still no answer. A louder knock got no answer so we decided to go around to the back of the house to the Chief's bedroom window. It was smoky and unwashed. There were no curtains to obstruct our view.

There lay the Chief with his mouth wide open, snoring raucously in his bed close to the window. All of his lights were on as a man who had a million fears. The Chief's mouth was wide open as he shot snores across the room. A thin, white sheet laid unevenly across his mound shaped belly and streamed down the side of his sagging bed onto the floor. A myriad of mosquitoes and a host of other weird species including sausage flies all gathered around him while others played frantically about the light bulb above his head. I recall hearing the Chief saying once that he was immune to malaria.

Ekoko gave a light knock. "Oh, Chiefy, sah?"

It got his attention. He gave a spasmodic jerk.

"What? Who da hell?"

"It's Ekoko, Chief. I am with Mr. Holiday and Mr. Namme. Sorry to disturb you at this time of the night, sah, but we have something important to tell you."

"Why can't it wait until tomorrow? Can't you see dat I am in bed?" "I'm afraid that it can't wait until tomorrow. It is too urgent, sah."

"All right. All right. But it betta be dam good. Meet me around da front."

The bright overhead light flashed on. A key could be heard turning on the other side. The door opened slowly.

"Well?" came the unpleasant voice.

"Uh, Chief, may we borrow your shovel sah?"

The Chief exploded. "You idiot," he yelled. "You call me from my peaceful sleep just to ask me for a damn shovel? Has part of your brain taken a leave of absence?"

"Oh, uh, no sah, Namme said. "Mr. Holiday's wife had her baby today but unfortunately, the child died tonight. We thought that you should be the first to officially know about it. We need the spade to bury the baby."

The Chief gave no condolences, as I had not expected him to. He closed the door while we waited.

A few minutes later the door opened slightly and a short, fat, black arm abruptly shoved a rusty spade with a crooked wooden handle into Namme's startled face. The door shut and the overhead light went out.

"My heavens," Ekoko said after he left the Chief's compound. "Did you notice the Chief's cold actions?"

"Indeed I did," replied Namme. "I thought at least that he would show some feelings of sympathy. If I hadn't caught this spade when I did, he would have hit me in the face with it."

They both looked at me and said at the same time: "Sorry, Mr. Holiday, we cannot speak for the actions of others."

I knew that the Chief was still angry about our clash. He had it out for me since the day that I crossed him. I knew that it could get worse. It simply had to get worse.

Again we started on our two hour journey by foot to the college. We finally reached my house.

"Mr. Namme, hold my baby," .

"Where are you going, sah?" Ekoko asked.

"To get two lights from my house," I explained. I came back from the house with my Bible, a torch and a photograph of the baby's mother and I.

"But sah," exclaimed Namme, "I thought you were bringing two lights."

"I did, Mr. Namme. I brought my Bible and a torch. The brightest light is the Word of God."

"A very wise saying, sah." Ekoko exclaimed.

He had already began digging the grave. In Africa, for a small child, only three and a half feet is required, but because of the vermin, with their keen sense of smell, they always dig them a little deeper. It was decided that the body should be buried very near my house. By custom, I was to be the first person to shovel the dirt, although Ekoko had started digging. He gave the spade to me while he held the body, and I began digging the grave for my son. The photograph of his mother and I would be placed in it beside him.

I completed the digging with my hands. I came to a rock. Namme quickly fell to his knees and helped me tug at it until it was loose. As I thought about it, it became more over whelming. My African brothers in this part of the continent had accepted me as one of their very own, even a part of the African's bitter experience. No matter where I would go from there, I would always have a part of me buried beneath the African soil, the soil that my ancestors walked on before they were taken away in chains and it was the soil consecrated by the innocence of so many African babies, like my little Silhouette, whose's body lies resting beneath it.

"Whew, there it is," Namme exclaimed with relief. "Just about deep enough."

I stooped down and placed the body in the grave.

"Now shall we read a few words from the Bible before we cover the body?" Ekoko asked.

I handed him the book and held the light on its pages for him. He turned to Job the fourteenth chapter and read, "Man that is born of a woman is of a few days and full of trouble. He cometh forth like a flower and is cut down. He fleeth also as a shadow and continueth not."

After reading, he closed the book and said, "We know not, little one, what ill wind brought you our way, but we pray that it will carry you on to a much better place. You never meant to stay with us. Neither did you mean to break our hearts by leaving us, but you were traveling on a journey and for some reason you decided to stop by and pay us a visit. This has all come about because there is Some One who is far wiser than we, Who decided that you should follow Him. The Lord giveth and the Lord taketh away. Blessed be the name of the Lord."

I laid the photograph on the tiny bundle. According to custom I cast the first spade of dirt on the body, then turned and walked away into the night while the two humble men completed the burial.

CHAPTER 26

THE DRUMS

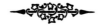

No newcomer can lie still at night and listen to the ubiquitous pounding of the distant African drums and not be stirred by their mysterious rhythm to search for their sources. Only this time, as I lay restlessly in the house, the drums sounded different. They had a tempo that I had not been accustomed to hearing.

It was in the darkness of the early morning and with Carol still far away at the clinic, and in the aftermath of Silhouette's death, sleep was impossible for me. I needed a different kind of experience, one that was profound enough to shake me out of my remorseful gloom the kind of impact that would challenge the bittersweet torture of the African saga that plays itself out in the drudgery of everyday life.

, *Tonight,* I thought, *I will find those drums!*

I got up, dressed, grabbed my stout walking stick and headed toward the dense forest. I must admit that it was not the wisest thing to do, especially if you are traveling alone. The "quest for adventure" in my blood rang out to me again. I have followed God through many unwelcome places and someday the quest for adventure will lead me to follow Him through the valley of the shadow of death, and by faith in his All-powerful Yeshua I will wait for Him until He returns to stand me back again upon my feet.

The moon was unusually bright, casting its pleasant hue on the campus. I would still need the walking stick to beat the ground in front of me to chase away the cobras that could be heard slithering through the tall grass. Most Africans simply give no thought to it but it was my unforgettable experience with the deadly Mamba that nearly cost my life. I would never again go about without my trusty stick.

The school campus seemed strangely silent as I walked across it. Not a light from a candle or lantern could be seen coming from the dormitory windows. It did appear a bit suspicious but I assumed that everyone was sound asleep.

Since the student's behavior was so impeccable, there really wasn't any assumptions left to be concerned about. The pigs were startled when they heard me. They scrambled to their feet, no doubt expecting that I had brought them some food. The further I walked into the forest, the more relentless the drums pounded. With a thunderous beckoning they sounded on and on. It could have actually been the heartbeat of Africa, and it seemed that if the drummers had stopped the beating, they too would have died.

With the campus far behind me, I had walked about forty five minutes into the forest. I quashed the notion to turn back. It was too late. I was almost there. I had to see the thundering heart of Africa. I saw a fire in the distance. At last, I had found the source. They actually did shake the atmosphere like a monstrous heart beat, as if the thunders of heaven had descended.

As I approached the edge of the forest where there was a clearing. To my surprise, there were the students, nearly all of them. The girls were nearly naked and the boys were thinly clad as well. They wore nothing more than strips of cloth that hardly covered their genitals. All were dancing and chanted loudly and harmoniously in their native language.

I stood behind a tree, as close as I could without being noticed. I was not supposed to be there. It was not for my eyes to see. The forest belonged to them. The campus was the Chief's. Tonight they would have their say, only this time in ritual. As the drums resounded, the boys danced with cutlasses in their hands. A huge bonfire leaped from the center of their circle. Near it stood a large, well-crafted effigy of a pig.

When the boys danced near the effigy, each one took his turn at swiping at it. The message was clear. The glow of the roaring fire painted their black skins with a tint of polished copper. Shining bodies cast huge shadows that silhouetted the surrounding forest with the mimic of shimmering phantoms. Beads of sweat rushed profusely down as they stomped and fell to the soggy earth that evidenced it. The entire scene was intensified by the arousing odor of musk, African musk, accentuated by the saturation of the sweet blend that rose from the burning forest ebony.

The captivating lure of that unforgettable redolence spawns a craving that is unique to Africa. The dance itself was mesmerizing. It was a vortex with an irresistible compulsion. The artistic beauty of voluptuous twisting and shaking with the irresistible power that was overwhelming enough to topple the most ridged sentinels of abstinence and send them soaring into the void of their forbidden imaginations with the craving to reach out and grasp the feel of life itself and bring it by the hand back into the realm of reality's desire to fall in love with someone or something that you will never live to see.

I was as close as a man could venture out into the forest clearing without being swept up and conveyed to the highest summit, bathed with an ecstasy where there were no other passions left to be desired.

It was a part of Africa that the wildest dreams may never know, over flowing the capacities of human containment, leaving it exhausted at the edge of that ulotricious hairline with more than enough that a man could possibly beg for, even if he desired as a fool, to repeat it over again. A sweet madness that welcomed his insanity with the one deep breath of the black romance that spans two continents.

The students were never more serious than they were that night. It was certainly not a motivational dance. They had been on fire for quite some time. It was a dance for revenge. They would be bathed in the smoke of fire, continue on carrying it's odor on their bodies as a reminder to execute their plans as sons and daughters of the fire of destruction. The inevitable had now arrived to be unfolded in reckless discord.

CHAPTER 27

THE RIOT

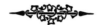

It was the night that all hell would break loose. Every student was on the alert. That day they attended their studies and afterward they carried out their hard labor as Chief Omubu insisted. There were days in the past when he had worked them until some of them would pass out from exhaustion, mostly from under nourishment, but all of this was about to come to a screeching halt.

On this particular evening, the Chief had left the school for his home, but had planned to return to finish his affairs. Among those concerns would be his major priority of seeing to it that his darling pigs were well tended to, stuffing them with corn maize and appeasing them with wine. I suppose that it was his way of "tucking them in" until the morning. In either case, it would leave the area reeking with palm wine mingled with pig's poop, something obnoxiously un-pleasant to attempt to sleep by.

There is an ancient proverb that was spoken in irony by the wicked King Ahab, yet, there is a lesson that may be learned from it "Let not the man who puts on his sword boast like him who takes his off."

That advice was an omen of woe to an unwise man such as the Chief, who had taken for granted every one hundred thousand heart beat days of his life.

The teachers, up to this time had not been paid their salaries. They were so angry that nothing else mattered any more. Strangely enough, they had no idea about the student's plan but they too had plans of their own. Theirs was the decision to go on strike the following day. How would they do it since worker's unions are not tolerated in Africa?

They would simply not show up for work. They would be conspicuously absent.

The students wanted to be sure that there would be no witnesses around when they carried out their plan. They warned the Night Watchman that there would be some kind of trouble on the campus and that it wouldn't be wise for him to stay around. The man made no protest about it, and absconded.

Tonight, it was to be the majority rule where havoc would reign and there would not be anyone to stop it. The extent of what was about to occur would be intentionally unpredictable, even for the safety of human life, there would be no guarantee.

I had just taken my nightly splash from the last bit of water left in the bucket. I climbed into bed. While lying there I gazed up at my stiff tailed audience that watched me with beady eyes from the overhead rafters, I blew out the candle and threw the sheet over my head to keep the mosquitoes guessing. No sooner had I closed my eyes that I heard what sounded like a window being shattered, but because I was fairly exhausted, I didn't give it much thought.

Again, there was another loud crash which sounded as if a door had fallen. This was followed by another window being shattered.

"A riot!" I thought. It was reminiscent of the Black high school students in Soweto protesting months earlier in South Africa against the Afrikaans.

There was a sudden pounding on my door.

"Mista Holiday. Please open door, quickly."

I hesitated, not wanting to take any chances. Again there was pounding, this time more furiously.

"Please, sah. I've something urgent to tell you."

At this, I swung the door opened and there stood a Mr. Tanyi Stevens, another young colleague. He was a bloody spectacle and nearly out of breath. As he tried to squeeze out his words, blood trickled down is face. His shirt was torn to shreds. There was sheer panic in his desperate eyes.

"Sah, you must leave quickly. The students are rioting. They have gone completely mad. The boys, the girls, all of them!"

I snatched up my trousers and shirt and rushed out of the back of the house in my shorts. After putting them on in the bushes, Tanyi and I hurriedly made our way through the coffee plantation next to the school and onto MBonge Road. We made sure that we had cleared the area.

"Tell me, Tanyi, what happened back there?"

Tanyi paused to catch his breath. He was trembling as he spoke.

"I was in the Form Four study room, sah. Everything seemed so peaceful and quiet. Suddenly, a chap just opened up his desk and brought out a rock and without any warning, he hurled it through the window. He then cried, "Onward, Comrades!, Onwards Fight to the death!" He then said something about "Death to Mister Jones and his men!" I have no idea what that meant."

"I have an idea" I answered. "But go on."

"Well, sah, It just so happened that somebody picked up a lantern and whether it was intentional or not, I don't know, but just as I turned around, they smashed me on my head. As I was trying to get away, a group of boys grabbed me by my shirt and began ripping it nearly off of me. It all happened so suddenly that before I knew it, the students had blown out their candles, dashed kerosene everywhere and threw their lanterns on the floor. I could hear the doors in the other classrooms being knocked down chairs and desk were being chopped up. I was hit twice again in the head as I was struggling like hell to get away. How I managed, sah, was a miracle."

Tanyi and I looked back in the school's direction. The night sky lit up from the blazing buildings.

"Somebody might be hurt back there." I said as I started back toward the school. Tanyi grabbed me by the arm.

"Wait, sah, where are you going?"

"Back to the school, someone could be hurt!"

Tanyi looked at me in dismay. "Have you gone mad,

sah? I know these people. They are no longer human be-ings. They are demons out of control. I beg you, sah. Don't go back there. They would never listen to you. They are too angry. They would only kill you."

"Did you warn the Headmistress?" I asked.

Tanyi gave me that strange look, as if to say, "You have got to be kidding me."

"There was no need to go to her house, sah. She lives very near the girl's dorm, but those students would never bother to harm her. She is a part of this plot."

"Are you sure of that?" I asked. I suspected it all along.

"I am so sure, sah. Very sure," he answered convincingly.

"Let's alert the Chief," I said, "and from there to find the gendarmes."

Tanyi and I ran along the road. We stopped once to look behind us. The fire was much larger. It sent up a roar that could be heard for miles. The frenzy cries of the students competed against it. The villagers who had been awakened were now running toward it all, in our opposite direction.

After about two miles, we saw two bright head lights ap-proaching us. It was the Chief. He was unaware of the riot and was headed back to the College. We waved him down. Normally, he would have passed us by, leaving dust in our faces, but he must have noticed how frantic we were that caused him to skid abruptly as he came to a stop.

"Chief, the students are rioting," Tanyi shouted.

When Omubu heard these words, we could see his face against the panel lights of his car. Sheer panic had taken over.

"It tis you, Holiday," he cried as he pointed his stubby finger in my face. "You are behind dis, I will have you jailed fa dis and aftawads deported."

"No, Chief, no, Holiday is not the one! Tanyi spoke up. "It is the Headmistress. She is the one."

The chief looked at me. His eyes lowered. Tanyi had persuaded him. He was no doubt sold on those assumptions rather than on me, because of his long time battles with her.

Suddenly, it all seem to hit the Chief like a ton of bricks. "My pigs!" he yelled. "I must go home and get my gun." He attempted to turn the car around. "My pigs, dey will all be killed."

"No, Chief," I urged."There may be some teachers and perhaps some innocent students that could be trapped in there. By this time, there could be some casualties. Who knows, some could already be killed. Besides. there may be some of your relatives there."

The dialogue among the three of us was over in a matter of seconds but it seem to mean nothing to the Chief. Finally Tanyi suggested. "You must drive to the SDO's (Senior District officer) office, sah. He is the only man who can stop the riot."

"Yis, yis," The Chief agreed. "I must get to de SDO. He's de only one," he said.

This, I recall, was one of the few instances during the entire time that I had known the Chief that he was willing to accept anyone's advice. There are times when in desperate moments a man may become clay in another man's hands but the molding should be by God.

How it happened that the SDO was alerted so soon about the riot was beyond me but he had ordered his policeman and a few gendarmes to proceed toward to the college ahead of him.

They would have to travel for several miles and since there were no fire departments in the area, the chances were that the fire would have ran its course.

The gendarmes passed by the Chief as he was in route to their headquarters. The Chief made a U turn and followed behind them. By the time that they arrived at the school, the fire had become so intense and was so wide spread that none of them could enter the campus. The students were between them and the burning buildings. They could only set out on the MBonge Road, watch it all in disbelief and wait it out until daybreak.

Some of the officials saw it all as "sweet revenge!" They were aware of the Chief's dastardly history, especially of his incident with the country's Parliament. The officers had a strong sense of patriotism. From the day that the Chief had hurled those insults at the seat of the government, the local authorities had been ordered to keep an eye on him, especially his handling any large transactions of money. This would account for their responsive neutrality with regard to his present loss of property. They had also received numerous complaints from various people who had brought grievances to them concerning the Chief. Over the years his unpaid debt had mounted.

Others complained of his stealing their property and what was worse, there were several of them who suspected him of committing homicide by cobra and Black Mamba. Although the latter allegations were never proven, the frequent threats from the Chief were always inclusive, involving these creatures as his agents.

Upon arriving at the school, the Chief drove beside the policemen. He hastily shifted and twisted to squeeze from beneath the steering wheel. The policemen saw him but said nothing.

"Why are you just standing deya?" he bellowed. The men were deaf to the Chief. They despised him. They were not about to jump at his roars. They took orders only from their superiors.

"Did you not hear me?" "How much louder do I have to ask you to get a response?"

Still, no answer. They remained rigid, not even a sympathetic glance from them. The furious Chief paraded back and forth in front them.

"Those students," he cried as he pointed toward the school. "They have destroyed my property! I have pigs in deya. Go in and stop dem, you idiots. It's your job. Where is your Captain?" The chief focused his attention on an officer of a lower rank. "I should known betta dan to have ask you," he exclaimed as he eyed the man up and down with disdain. "You have no rank." He began to interrogate the officer. "Now, I ask you again. Where is your Captain?"

Finally, from the back ground of a roaring fire, a solemn voice spoke out. "I am here, Chief." The Captain arrived and showed no more excitement than his men.

"Captain," yelled the Chief, pointing his finger at him.

"Order your men to go in and stop this madness. Round up those students and punish dem now. Look dey have destroyed my property. Look."

The Captain, still calm in spite of the Chief's raging insistence, gave him a stern look before speaking.

"There is absolutely nothing that we can do about it tonight, sah, absolutely nothing. You will just have to wait it out until tomorrow."

"But why?" ask the Chief pitifully.

"Chief," said the Captain. "I will not risk my men's lives nor will I order them to open fire on those students for the sake of your pigs. Besides, your school has no electricity, no water to fight those flames and we are not sure of what weapons those students might have. Furthermore, Chief, we cannot just go into the college beating up students. The innocent ones might get hurt. We will not make a move, sah, until there is daylight," he insisted firmly. "That is when we will be able to make an assessment."

"Make an assessment!?" screamed the Chief. "An assessment!?" He turned to the crowd, no doubt for support. "Are my two ears failing me? I can't believe what I have just heard dis man say, 'Assessment!' he says. Did I hear dis man correctly?' While my school is going up in flames, dis Captain heya is talking assessments." The Chief turned back to the Captain. "Captain, has it ever occurred to you dat if you wait until tomorrow, deya won't be a dam ting to assess?" At this, the Chief decided that he would make a move on his own.

"Where are you going, Chief?" asked the Captain.

"If you won't go in der," the Chief exclaimed, "en I'll do it myself!"

The Captain calmly stepped in front of the Chief. "Sorry, Chief. I can't allow you to go in there. If you value your life, you will remain here with us. If you should insist on doing so, I will not be held accountable for what should happen to you. I will simply have my Sergeant to fill out an I Told You So Form, and we will just walk away."

The light from the roaring flames showed the Chief's face. At last there was water in his angry eyes. Whether those tears were caused by fire light, the smoke, his anger, or even from remorse over his pigs, no one may ever know, but any man who is being crushed by the weight of heaven above and suppressed by the gauntlet of hell below will have no other recourse than to yield his harvest of tears. No man can spit into the face of heaven without discovering that gravity, being on heaven's side, will return its splatter into his face.

The Captain turned, facing the Chief in disgust. He was trying his best to see if there was at least an inkling of human compassion somewhere hidden within the deep, unexplored recesses of this man's soul. Was there a spark of insanity, psychopathic callousness, a core of undiluted ignorance imprisoned behind bars of manipulative genius? How did he get from the Parliament to a pig pen? Was it all by choice or as destiny would have it?

"Aren't your students of more importance to you, Chief, than your pigs?" He asked. "Sorry, Chief tonight, your pigs will have to wait,"

After about four hours, the shouts of the rioters ceased.

Only a few solitary yells could be heard.

"Comrades, Napoleon, Squealer, Victory."

Most of the students were now hid in the forest, out of sight. The fire eventually died out leaving a sickening smell of flesh in the smoky air. Finally, there was nothing more to hear. Everyone was exhausted from watching the blaze throughout the night and the morning. The policemen slept on the ground, clinging close to their weapons.

For whatever reason, the Captain was in a provocative mode, so he decided to probe a bit deeper into the Chief's past affairs. He saw how bitter the Chief was at this time, as he watched him grieve over his losses, so he decided to rub it in a bit more.

"By the way Chief, where did you acquire all of the monies to purchase all of this property? He asked. The Chief exploded.

"I stole it!" he screamed furiously. "How in de hell do you tink I got it? I stole it all!" When the police and the gendarmes heard this remark, they all burst out laughing hysterically, some even rolling on the ground.

The Chief, under jurist prudence, certainly could not be prosecuted on his own testimony, but it was a gratifying stab in his side on the Captain's part.

CHAPTER 28

A MOURNER OF SWINE

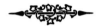

That morning a bulging red sun slowly rose on a silent, devastated college. All was in ruins. The fire spared nothing. An act of nature could not have caused any worse havoc. From the extent of the damages, it could be clearly seen that a malicious plan had a hand in it. Any passing stranger would have sworn that it was caused by a single act of divine judgment. A few scattered embers and the narrow spirals of smoke were faint reminders of the roaring conflagration. The drowsy policemen and gendarmes who had rested on the ground and slept in their vehicles rose to their feet at their sergeant's command. They were given a brief "search plan" by the Captain and were given strict orders not to fire their weapons. They would have to step across broken glass, mattresses torn to shreds and then burned.

The aluminum roofs that had not been ripped off were bent so far backward that one would have thought that it had been done by a power machine. Rocks, mud clods, iron bars and sticks covered the sagging, punctured roofs that remained. Those sand and mud brick buildings that the Chief had put up by student labor were leveled to the ground and the broken walls that were left standing were laden with obscene drawings and threats of death, all smudged and written with charcoal. A few of the teacher's names had also been written on them.

The students had dashed kerosene against every building. As devastating as it was and so sinisterly crafted, it was a masterful piece of macabre work. There was something to be said about an incendiary maniacal twisting of a revengeful enthusiast, who was hell-bent on nothing less than total destruction and insinuating nothing other than his obvious intentions.

There were crowds of people from the surrounding villages that stood motionless, gazing in shock at the heap of charred ruins. Some of them brought their pots and pans, waiting to rush in and squabble over anything salvageable. Large flocks of vultures, attracted by the smell of the carnage, had already begun to circle overhead.

The students kept silent. Most of them stayed hidden in the forest. Once in a while, a designated lookout could be seen peeking from behind a tree. Some of them studied the officials from as close as behind a ruined building. All were afraid, trembling. Although they knew about the unpredictability of African soldiers, they were not aware of the Captain's orders for his men to stand down. Already, a wild rumor had gotten out that the gendarmes were given the orders to execute extreme violence and that they were about to penetrate the forest and flush out the culprits.

Some of the students complicated matters by going further back into the never ending forest. Most of the utensils and pots that were lying about had been used for latrines. Signs were written on them: "Today, we have toilets." The word "beans!" was written on the kitchen door that laid on the ground.

The Headmistress joined us with a solemn expression as we walked on to the campus accompanied by the officials. It would have to be concluded that it did appear suspect to see her house intact, as it stood so close by the dormitories.

Chief Omubu broke through the ranks of the officers. He began all over again yelling and screaming, cursing in his native language. He hurried as fast as his short legs could carry him over to what was once the Main Office building.

"It's ruined!" he cried as he pounded furiously on the remaining side of the charred structure. "My buildings, dey are totally ruined!" At his feet laid the petty cash box open, and one or two documents that escaped the flames.

"Dey have destroyed de accounts!" He shouted as he crumbled the papers in his hands. "But dey won't get ta way without paying de fees in arrears!" "I will squeeze it out of der black skins! every franc of it, even if I have to sit down on my own black oss and cello tape des dam papas togetha, piece by piece. I will do it!"

On his way to the piggery, the Chief noticed what used to be the adjoining library. Not a single book had been spared. All were burned as well. The library door stood by itself between its supports. On it was written, "Send the books back to the Queen!"

"Captain!" shouted the Chief. Look at my library, scattered to da wind!"

He rushed over to another sign.On it was written something which caused the Chief to place both of his hands flat against the wall and nearly burst into flames. It read, "Long live the HM, Omubu is a tyrant, Death to Mr. Jones, Victory for his slaves."

"Aha!" he cried, pointing to Mrs. Diop. "You are responsible for dis whole ting! I knew it all along! You were de masta mind behind it all. Dat sign on de wall is living proof. They no longer respect me as Head of dis college!"

The Headmistress trembled. Her face turned red. All eyes were on her.

"That is not true, Chief," she answered. "Why would you say a thing like that?

"It had to be you!" interrupted the Chief. "I've see de way that you have been wooing dey stu…." He then turned to the Captain. "Take dis woman to prison. She has been planning dis sabotage for a long time. She told me to my face dat I was not fit to run a school."

The captain walked over and abruptly raised the palm of his hand toward the Chief. "Now, now, Chief, he warned. "Don't start making accusations until you're sure of what you are saying. And I might remind you, sah, those are serious allegations that you are making. You can't just go around accusing people unless you have proof."

The Chief then turned to Ekoko. "Sound de assembly bell!" He ordered. "Tell dem to come out of hiding."

Ekoko looked at the Chief and exclaimed, "But Chief,

we have no more assembly bell. It has disappeared."

"Well. Sound de dam drums!"

"But Chief, there are no drums."

"Well, run into de forest, you idiot, and start yelling for dem and stop making assembly excuses!"

The Captain stopped Mr. Ekoko.

"Wait!" he said. He snatched the loud speaker out of an officer's hand and shouted toward the forest. "Attention, all students, including those of you who are hiding in the bush. This is your Senior District Officer speaking."

All was quiet, except for the squawking of the vultures above.

"I have not come here to harm you." The Captain repeated this over again.

A few of the very young students that had been shoved out into the clearing by their older classmates crept forward timidly. The Captain observed their shattered appearance. The girls began sobbing loudly. The Captain spoke again.

"Although I have given my officers the authority to keep the peace at all cost, even at the cost of your lives." He waited, then spoke "But when I see what I am seeing, I see sadness, hunger, and I see that you are frightened. I do not see you students as anarchists and rioters. Instead, I see you as my very own children, as my own sons and daughters. You may come out. Don't be afraid. I give you my word."

These soothing words from the SDO brought a sigh of relief to the intense crowd. Some of them had sons and daughters in that forest.

The Captain clearly demonstrated a text book example

of how a leader should conduct his affairs. Contrary to the unforgettable classical and even a few contemporary fascist or totalitarians whose hallucinating paranoia is the only source for his evil ideology that he has crammed down the gagging throats of the weary masses.

Were some of these students worthy of punishment? The answer is "yes" but there was no crime that was worthy of death. For the most part, they were students that needed to be fed, respected, educated and taught the laws of the land. America's Educational system could also mandate the revised codes of their various states into the earliest stages of their curriculums.

The Captain spoke again to the students."There is a way for us to settle our disputes and grievances," he said looking about him, even at his men. It was a caution to those whom he knew to be trigger happy. He continued. "But you have gone about it the wrong way. We all know part of your troubles that you have had here at the college. We have known it for a long time. And believe me, your Government is going to investigate those that are responsible. But you must never forget that we are Africans, and we must settle our differences as Africans.

The Captain held up his rifle. "Not with these weapons, taking people's lives, destroying their property, as it was done in such an un-African way in Rwanda, Uganda where blood was the nectar of fools."

Good for the Captain a leader quite the contrary to the Chief. He showed them that leadership as well as a discipline that was commendable and that leaders, all leaders must be men of great compassion. He had shown that justice does not walk this earth alone. It has a companion. Justice walks with mercy. That will be the very last thing that any man will ever need when his last breath abandons his body, Mercy and Breath vaporizes. Mercy is everlasting. Without mercy, a man is hurled out into the garbage pit of eternity with his unrepentant luggage following him.

How synthetic is our human justice. How alternative it is to the genuineness of the Divine justice that we have access to every day of our busy lives. Superficial justice is as close as a man can get to evil without actually identifying with it. We have assigned it to accomplish our "dirty work." It is so subtle that it can slip past the weary sentinels who are exhausted from battles and weakened with compromise. That is why we often feel contaminated and angry with ourselves because we have finally realized that we have compromised with evil. We have invited evil into our homes and given it a guest room and when it over stays its welcome, we can't put it out. Instead of destroying evil, we simply put it to rest.

False justice has crept into our society, word by word, reform by reform, ideology by ideology until finally our entire culture has unrecognizably transformed. Now justice stands before us blind folded, using only its ears to determine what is to be right or evil. True justice has no blind fold because it is God's perfect judgment over all men's actions. Again, the herald goes forth and cries aloud "Truth has fallen in the streets of the continents of this world and equity stands far off!"

If the moral sentinels of mankind had been invaded by a visible army of deception, they would have no doubt fought them to the death. Most would have willingly gone down in history as Martyrs, but Satan is aware that Martyrs never die. Their names live on, and the magnitude of their glory continue to swell. They are memorialized on monuments, acknowledged by valedictorians, and indelible in slogans. Martyrdom speaks loudly. It makes an outward declaration and exposes the evil. This is why Satan hates it with such passion.

On the other hand, it is deception that creeps in and destroys from within. We are reminded of the ancient words of Yeshua "But know this, that if the good man of the house had known in what watch the thief would come, he would have watched, and would not have suffered his house to be broken up."

Perhaps we should take a second look at our nations and ask ourselves, "Are we living in a house of cards? Are we the next to fall?

It is on that same note that I am compelled to mention that Tribalism in Africa and racism in American will never be swept across their thresholds and into their surrounding seas. And neither will it ever be written on our tomb tones: "Here lies a noble racist," For these two evils were also born of ideological rape.

The Captain turned. "I want to see all of the staff and the School Prefects in the stadium area immediately."

He then turned and said, "and you also, Chief."

All heads turned to look for Chief Omubu. The Captain

called out again "Chief Omubu." There was no answer. "Has anybody seen the Chief?" he asked.

A voice in the distance yelled out, "There is the chief, sah, over there !"

More than five hundred people followed the Captain. Suddenly, everyone came to a halt.

There he was the Chief, a short, stubby figure of a man, now even lower. He had fallen down on both his knees inside of the piggery with both of his hands sunk in the oozing muck up to his elbows. He was loudly sobbing profusely. Totally oblivious to the on lookers who could not believe their eyes nor their ears. He had already smeared his face with the mud that was mingled with feces and blood. He slowly raised himself up and placed both of his hands to the sides of his head.

All of his pigs had been slaughtered, totally mutilated, even to the smallest of them. Not one had been spared. The huge boar was barely alive as he laid gasping for breath. The Chief watched in horror as it made its last spasmodic jerks and listened to its faint death-squeals.

The crowd moved in to get a closer look. A few of them looked a bit sad. The pigs laid scattered about and swollen, releasing an even worse putrefied stench. The miasma of it all was sickening. Coagulated pools of blood, battered pigs, swollen with bloody mucus dangling from their snouts. Besides being swollen from the increasing heat and armies of maggots, a myriad of flies swarmed their bodies and clang tenaciously to the Chief's back and arms like a mourning garment. Sharp stakes were driven into their sides, hearts, stomachs, and necks. Their throats were slashed from ear to ear. No sight had ever been ghastlier.

The Chief was still buckled to his knees in utter defeat, wailing and lamenting his beloved swine. His tears mingled with the sweat that poured from his vitreous eyes. Dark, heavy stains of blood that had absorbed into his royal gown crept up inch by inch until they reached his tubby waist. He looked through briny tears at his prize boar that laid its breathing had grown fainter, and before a gazing crowd he cried "Papa Childs, What did dey do to you!?" While still on his knees, he made his way over to another one. "My poor, poor Fumiy, Motha pig!" He crawled over to another. "Fumyta, Fumyta, you can no longer show me a Wanda! Tesima!, Pesimdo!, Mebbi!, and all of my little ones, gone, gone fa ev-vah!"

He looked at the crowd and screamed at the top of his voice. "Just look at what you have done! Why did you kill my pigs? What have dey done to you? I will find de culprits who did dis ting to me, even if I have to consult every juju man in de kontry "You will pay fa dis, all of you! I am Chief Victor Omubu, Chief of all Ijo Batanga!. I will neva let you rest. I will summons de lightning. I will call de thunder. I will send my cobras into your huts. I will have my re-venge, even if I have to sell my royal navel cord to de devil. Whatever it takes, I will revenge de death of my pigs!"

The students and the crowds stood with their mouths opened in utter shock at the Chief's terrifying words. They took the threats of witchcraft seriously. The Captain and his officers looked at each other in dismay. They shook their heads in pity.

"I cannot believe what I have just heard or seen for that matter." He said. "Here is a man who cares nothing at all for his people, who have suffered so severely by his hand, yet he has become a mourner of swine!"

I too, recall the many times that I watched the Chief in unbelief, as he stood in his favorite spot beneath the thick banana leaves as he eyed his pigs and watched them grow, glut, and multiply. I watched him praise them and pour out magnanimous libations of wine. Perhaps he was captured by them because their natures were so identical.

In the earliest stages of his life, he had bonded with his pigs. The swine by their nature were gluttonous, and so was the Chief as well as impious. The swine were accustomed to wallowing in their own filth but the Chief felt justifiably content to wallow in the filth of immorality and callousness. The swine never stopped to look up until their food ran out and neither did the Chief look up to the God of heaven from whence came his blessings. The school was the Chief's pearl of great price but he did only as his pigs would have done. He simply trampled it under his feet.

END

ABOUT THE BOOK

A Mourner of Swine by Walter Brown

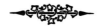

Set amongst the turmoil in South Africa in the 1970s, students from numerous Soweto schools began to protest in the streets in response to the introduction of Afrikaans as the medium of instruction in local schools. In *A Mourner of Swine* we will be swept into the life of a wealthy, shrewd and unscrupulous African Chief who holds the well-being of those students and teachers who are helpless about him, within the clutches of his greedy hands.

Walter Brown is a retired minister living in the Northwest of Washington State. *A Mourner of Swine* is based on his experiences after living in Central Africa in the 1970s.

The author once read of how Dr. Paul Scherer told of Sir Francis Drake's recruitment of sailors. "There sat the old salts on the rocky coasts of England telling the country lads not about the pleasures of the sea but of its dangers, its risk. They talked about the high waves and the stout winds and of gallant ships riding it out through mad euroclydones until those country boys were intoxicated with the quest of adventure. They wanted it so much so that they would run away from home to become a part of it."

The author knew that this was the stuff that he, like most men are made of. "It's not the fear of the unknown," he would say, "but the challenge of the unknown. You will know me better by the outcome of my experiences with the unknown challenges ...even if I failed. Do not be afraid to take the fear out of risk. Fear is for men who have the time for it. It may be in their best interest, perhaps their best ally, but an ally has an uncertain longevity. It can be around for minutes, days, or even years.

As for the author, he says, "God has not given me the spirit of fear but of a sound mind."

This story speaks of the author's ardor for black consciousness but always within the framework of biblical morality.

Yes, "global naïveté" the author believes the last time it was seen lying wounded across the paths of history's eroding assumptions, but as it goes with many true events, as this one is based on, is hopefully with lessons to profit by... never really stopping where it all began but simply the door to a ramified version confronting more people and similar events.

There will always be others who will cast themselves into the same role, as did their chagrined predecessors, acting out identical scenarios, carbon copies as they may be with no cognizance of what has transpired before they had ever arrived. They too will temporarily grip the slimy scepter of human exploitation and hold it over the "damnable destiny" of others that they had conspired it to be, only to discover when it is too late, to their chagrined apocalypse, that they too were merely manipulated victims puppeteer by a far more sinister intelligence than themselves.

"Be what you say you are " he would comment, but be that with dignity, wisdom, truth, and by all means devoid of prejudices, hate and self-destructive anger. Show respect for all men. The world has no place for any race that despises another.

Speaking of truth, the writer often wonders how the destiny of America would have been shaped had the Constitution read "life, liberty, happiness, and the pursuit of Absolute Truth."

As far as Africa herself, there seem to forever remain within the author's sight a repulsive despondency over the appalling plight of what he describes as a "blanket of bedlam" which has settled down across the "dismal African night." For the most part, his environment in Africa is abhorrent and saturated with the miasma of sickness, the squalor of unquenchable neediness, and the looming phantom of heart- tearing infant mortality. The latter is expressed in the premature death of his own son, Silhouette, born and buried in Africa.

This all seems to foam out of a stagnant legacy of exploitation by foreign powers and a frigid apathy for humankind's well-being, but it is further enhanced by the most deplorable factor of all, an evil that the author has seen on both sides of the Atlantic, the black man's inhumanity to black men. Since the tragedy effects the lives of women and children, then it stands to reason that the entire race is traumatized.

Picture this black child standing by the grave of his father who some days ago was put there by another black man.

Just recently, an article from a newspaper set off tremors across the Facebook

"While blacks are just 12.6% of the nation's population they're roughly half of people murdered in this country each year. The vast majority of these killings are at the hands of other blacks." The article went on to say, "If that doesn't shock you, maybe this will; more blacks were murdered in the USA in 2009 alone than all the US troops killed in the Iraq and Afghanistan wars together."

In Africa the author calls it "inverted apartheid" with nothing to gain, counterproductive to all concerned. In America, he labels it "a deliberate evil with a blind agenda to close the book on the history of a race. Like the Mayans and the Aztecs... a crazed apathy for blood lust, a penchant loyalty to self-destruct."

Therefore, the question is asked, "What should the black man do about it all?" Well, the American black man will have to do a little forensic in retrospect. He must go back through the dust-covered isles of his own past. He must recall that he was not brought to James Town as an illegal alien and certainly not as a special guest on "His Majesty's Service." The black man was brought here under the false premise that he was a genetically inferior race to those who sold him, to those who hefted his testicles on the auction blocks and bought him. In certain cases the black man was actually sold from Africa by his own conniving blood relatives who thought that a piece of red cloth was better than he was.

Immediately after his emancipation, which took more than two hundred miserable years, he was not welcomed nor even grandfathered into the so-called "genetically superior club." After the Civil War, the black man was on his own (as he still is for the most part to this day) or at the mercy of the Native American Indian. Although at the time, the black man's physical prowess, which had developed over the years of hard labor, was an amenable asset for cheap labor.

However, it was not a recognizable accreditation that would be efficacious enough, in their thinking, to bring him out of the acclaimed sub-species category.

Sad to say, even to this day, there still exist on planet earth men who "warp" to this very norm with the tenacity of unbelievable ignorance. Such stagnate thinking exist in this twenty first century and is by far the largest quantity of absurdity that has ever stumbled across the stages of the anthropomorphic intellect, and should be searched through the nation's dockets and purged from the arteries of its academia.

Although the south is still crippled by the Civil War, (mental scars if nothing more), the African American never recovered from the scars of racism. It is quite unlikely that he, as a race, ever will. He is still within the wilderness of autonomy.

Unlike his Hispanic counterpart who was grandfathered into this nation at the number of eleven million, the black man did not have a powerful nation like the Vatican to back him up. Neither was he set on a course to complete the Vatican's agenda. Now that the Vatican has a Spanish speaking Pope, that agenda is becoming more apparent. It makes sense that the Hispanic would become an entrenched elite to be reckoned with in the brief duration of America's apostate history. The Hispanic is alive and well and it would not require very much encouragement on their part to continue as an integral entity.

We must not forget, however, that the Hispanic within the USA, is building upon the historical contribution of nation- building, long after the Emancipation that the black man earlier contributed to.

Again, the author ask, "What should the black man do about it all?" The most absurd idea for a solution, as one leader of a "Black Cult" had suggested, would be to create an autonomy of total separation from the white man and from the rest of the Americans. That was not God's plan from the beginning. To conceive of such a notion simply reveals its demonic origin.

Absolute race autonomy in America would never work for the black man. It worked for the Chinese because he had his own continent. However, what would the black man do with the thousands of blacks that populate the prisons of America? Would he build his own hospitals? In addition, upon whose soil? Who would protect him from the converging global genocidal organizations and government tolerated hate groups that are subsidized to fulfill their missions?

We must recall that the safest place for a slave was within his owner's real estate. The black man does not stand alone in this, because most of our country's citizens are indentured slaves.

How could he possibly allow himself to be denied white medical expertise?

From where would he draw his food source? There would be absolutely no educational system for his children. The armed forces would be all but black. Whom would he pay to defend his part of the country and with whose gold? Lastly, who would stand as a vanguard to be trusted in resisting another divide and conquer strategy by the races that live on the other side of those geographical boundaries?

To continue giving examples would be superfluous. It would only make for writing an Oscar worthy novel of ingenious nightmarish proportions, or it would be better described as a blistering essay in Valedictorian ignorance.

America is an extension of the ancient Roman Empire. It was there where slaves earned their freedom through gallantry, inventions, and even in literature. In America, the slaves earned an unrecognizable freedom through their hard labor. But now that the black man is free, there lies before him opportunities for gallantry, and a quixotic vision to work side by side for a "more perfect unity" among races.

The answer does not lie in another million man march. That effort solved nothing at all. It was too physical. Perhaps it has occurred to the American of African origin to inspire a nationwide, one year spiritual revival. Not a holiday but a soul searching revival.

There would be far more than a million man cry to the God of heaven. Such an effort would completely revolutionize and perhaps salvage what we have left as a culture. Moreover, it would set us on a spiritual quest that would be unprecedented since the cry of our slave ancestors.

There is a simple reminder that when the black man was emancipated, he had nothing material that he could boast of. He had no clothes, no food, no land, no transportation. But he did have his spirituality, the most powerful weapon that any race can have. In fact, he could be said to have been the spiritual conscience of America. Now we have sold it out for a tiny morsel of "nominal equal opportunity," and what is so deplorable is that we now have neither. Most of what we have replaced for it is an absurd quantity of harlequinism.

Such a movement with such a consensus would never go unsupported.

Men of every race under the sun would join the black man. Other nations abroad would kneel with us. It would not be every man to the god of his own liking, but back to the God that all of our ancestors once knew. The God that reminded us that there was a time on this earth when all of the biological progenitors knew exactly Who He was, and that He was the One and only true and living God, Who had revealed His self to the human race. (Romans 1: 21)

A revival of this proportion can be done because it has been done.

What was the extent of its power? What was the measure of its efficacy?

Go now, back into the hell of our darkest history and recall that it was not the slave revolts that struck terror into the hearts of the slave owners. Black uprisings occurred on an everyday basis. In fact, they were expected and prepared for. The inciters of those revolts were summarily dealt with and were made an example. He or she were rounded up and beaten within an inch of their lives. Either that or they were merely shot or hung, and the rest of the slaves were ordered back to work.

It was the prayers of the slaves that unnerved their masters. It was those same prayers that lifted the slaves into such an audience with God, that they were untrammeled by whips, bullets and blood hounds. The taskmasters could not hinder prayers. They could feel the supernatural presence of prayer all around them. They heard it in the fields, moaning as it blended in with the indistinguishable chant of the slaves, borne on the wings of the melancholy winds. Prayers were heard from the out houses. They were haunting when they were breathed in song from the slave quarters. Deep in the black of the night when black skins were absorbed in the dark when the slaves could not see each other, they rested their eyes on God. They were able to see Him by the fire that He placed on the altars of their hearts and God, to whom the darkness is as the light, saw and heard them.

It was there that the slaves which had been driven to the fringes of insanity that day as their heads pounded, their backs ached and their feet swollen. Their endurance had defied the fragile laws of mental cohesion, kneeled in an unconsolable anguish that liquefied into the pure gold by fervent prayers.

They poured out their request to God, to the very last dregs of their bleeding hearts. As they cried, their saliva congealed into membrane, as our Lord did when He cried out to his Father while hanging on the cross, membrane forming harp string stalactites from their tongues to the roofs of their mouths. They cried under the scorching sun and in zero winter, until it was made manifest to the world that Beauty has a mother whose name is Agony.

Why did it take so long for God to respond to the black man while in slavery? For the very same reason that it took Him so long to answer the Hebrews when they were in bondage. As a matter of fact, it took the black man far less time to be answered. The answer is because the longer that a race is in the furnace of affliction, she becomes a spiritual power to be reckoned with. The tyranny of slavery molded the black man into a spiritual entity for God's spiritual use.

As deplorable as it may have been, as a race, our luster since the Emancipation, has tarnished. That was not supposed to happen. Remember the slave gave the freedom of prayer back to God, and God, in return, answered them with freedom through prayer. It was effective enough for God to divide this nation. Just as He divided the Red Sea waters for the Hebrews to pass between. He also divided this nation for the black man to have a place of freedom, thereby dividing the North and the South. Through there, He walked us through the red sea of blood brought on by the Civil War.

Did it accomplish anything? Most certainly the freed men turned their faces up to God and shouted thanks to Him for responding so fervently to their fervent prayers.

God didn't care whether they smelled badly or if they had a poor mastery of English. He cared not whether their hair was curly or straight. God is in love with men's hearts. Come to Him and He will set you free from yourself.

It was not Abraham Lincoln but the God of Abraham who broke the chains of slavery. It was Jacob Thomas, an ex-slave who spoke of Lincoln's indifference: "I always thought a lot of Lincoln 'cause he had a heap of faith in de nigger ter think dat he could live on ' at all." The cry this time must be for freedom from the falsehoods of self-enslavement.

Deep within the very psychic of our race lies the hideous scars of racism. We are haunted by memories that we can't remember. Memories of dark days that we have never seen, a strangle vine hold that has somehow mutated and entangled. Has it become such a part of our hereditary ladder? Is it so embedded in our genes that we have accepted it as an alien host without question? Why should we live with an ancestral nightmare that springs from a historical reality that we have never experienced? Why such cannibalism, as seen in devouring our ethnic species? ...theft, drugs, down lowism, lethargic, depraved lifestyles that are designed to amputate what is left of black manhood?

A few independent blacks, though competent as some of them may be, cannot speak for the entire race.

We must all join in. The rich, middle class, the poor, the drug dealer, the prostitute, those behind prison bars, those

A MOURNER OF SWINE

within solitary confinement, those on death row, the intellectual, the illiterate.

All that have been mentioned were found in ancient Nineveh, an ancient Assyrian city on the eastern bank of the Tigris River. We all must cry out to Him whose way is in the whirlwind and who has to diminish His self to squeeze into His universe. America needs a people with a spiritual conscience. We were that once.

The paganizing infiltration of emerging churches have insulted the patristic ordinances. They have defied the ancient norms and have replaced them with a superficial spirituality that is oblivious to, yet practices, institutionalized depravity.

Nineveh was a Hammetic race of antiquity whose immoral stench had reached the nostrils of God, but through collective repentance through the preaching by a "whale swallowed Prophet. They escaped ground zero and received unhindered access to the grace of God.

Black men on both continents must learn from history to invest in the enhancement of each other and also, by all means, embrace the entirety of humanity, taking to heart that what one man needs, all men need. The basics of life, the inexhaustible treasure of unconditional love and a tear at the close of our lives. Hard core racism must not only be abandoned, but it must be banished to the Gehenna that spawned it. We must take its venom seriously and consider its spreading cancer within the universal society of the human race. We must embrace the age old truth that says, "No man liveth unto himself and no man dieth unto himself."

All of the elements of the aforementioned are personified in this true-life story, *A Mourner of Swine.*

Here, we will be swept into the life of a wealthy, shrewd, and unscrupulous African Chief who holds the well-being of those who are helpless about him within the clutches of his greedy hands.

Walter H. Brown

ABOUT THE AUTHOR

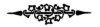

The Author's message is clear and is expressed with a colorful blend of historical honesty, political sobriety, poetical imagery and a plausible phase of romantic prose.

A Mourner of Swine, although centered within an African environment, sends its message across the imaginary, ethnic and cultural dimensions that has deterred our focus away from the expanding realities of our diminishing global village. A village that reminds us of just how small our planet really is. What is a threat to one man, is a threat to all men. Walter H. Brown sends out an invitation that he hopes will awaken the God-given dignity that slumbers within the bosom of a few.

This book is a call to the reader to reconsider the emergence of an alien radicalism that is devoid of values and whose purpose it is to destroy our attributes as men of compassion and to take up arms against the enemies of egotistical arrogances.

He is firmly convinced that a serious effort to eradicate empathy among one's own people and to expose the senselessness of toxic racism who's terminal germ begins at the core of society, can only be measured by the individual triumphs of the heart.

CPSIA information can be obtained
at www.ICGtesting.com
Printed in the USA
FSOW01n1107151117
41223FS